THE PANTHEISM
OF ALAN WATTS

DAVID K. CLARK

The King's Library

INTER-VARSITY PRESS
DOWNERS GROVE
ILLINOIS 60515

© 1978 by Inter-Varsity Christian
Fellowship of the United States of
America. All rights reserved.
No part of this book may be reproduced in
any form without written permission
from InterVarsity Press.

InterVarsity Press is the book publishing
division of Inter-Varsity Christian
Fellowship, a student movement active on campus
at hundreds of universities, colleges and
schools of nursing. For information
about local and regional activities, write IVCF,
233 Langdon Street, Madison, WI 53703.

Distributed in Canada through Inter-Varsity
Press-Canada, Unit 10, 1875 Leslie Street,
Toronto, Ontario M3B 2M5, Canada.

ISBN 0-87784-724-X
Library of Congress Catalog
Card Number:

Printed in the United States of America

FOREWORD

Rudyard Kipling said, "East is East and West is West and never the twain shall meet." Today it is not so, at least not with regard to Eastern philosophy and Western students. The invasion from the East has not yet reached apocalyptic proportions, but it is definitely on the increase. There are many reasons for this phenomenon, not the least of which is the spiritual vacuum created by the emptiness of Western materialism.

Now the pendulum is swinging back to the other extreme. Materialism declares that we are made happy by adding to our possessions. Thinking and, particularly, affluent young people know the vanity of this philosophy by experience. They often find themselves in the position of having everything to live with and nothing to live for. Out of this emptiness of spirit thousands of young people have turned from materialism to the other end of the spectrum, pantheism. By contrast pantheism proposes that we are made happy not by adding to our possessions but by taking away from our passions. Sadly enough, this extreme too is not self-fulfilling but literally self-destroying and futile.

Perhaps no one illustrates the futile pilgrimage of a Western mind into Eastern thought better than Alan Watts. It is for this reason that this excellent volume is overdue. It is a well-written and clearly reasoned analysis of one of the most important and influential Eastern philosophies today.

David Clark is particularly qualified to write this work. Born of Western parents but reared in the East (Japan) and trained in philosophy and religion, Mr. Clark has brought to bear both years of intensive research and extensive personal experience into an exciting volume on a crucial topic.

Norman L. Geisler
Trinity Evangelical Divinity School

1

INTRODUCTION

"Measuring and counting and weighing were invented very nicely to help us," wrote Plato. "Thus we are not ruled by appearance, . . . but by what has been counted and measured or even weighed." This line from *The Republic* reflects an attitude toward knowledge which has become dominant in Western culture. In our society speed, profitability, efficiency, logic, precision, accuracy and practicality overshadow aesthetic and spiritual values which also make up part of life. Much of Western culture still mirrors Plato's attitude: "That which trusts measure and reasoning would be the best part of the soul. . . . So that which goes contrary to this would be one of the inferior parts in us."[1]

A Challenge to the Status Quo
Rationalism, a thoroughgoing confidence in human reason, has led to discoveries of tremendous significance for humanity. Science has undeniably improved the physical quality of life on this planet. The world is a better place to live in, and reason and science have made it this way. So goes the stan-

dard, popular, seldom challenged analysis.

Now, however, many no longer consider science to be a near-divine discipline with the power to explain all of reality and build us a heaven on earth. Scattered modern critics of Western culture illustrate a growing tendency to reject science as the ultimate authority.[2]

Similarly, strict naturalism, a world view which holds that the universe is the result of natural, self-explanatory forces, is also losing some of its appeal. Confidence in science has been dampened by what may be a fatal flaw in strict naturalism as a world and life view. As Alan Watts the subject of this study, has observed, naturalists

often fail to recognize that their remarks about the universe apply also to themselves and their remarks. If the universe is meaningless, so is the statement that it is so. If this world is a vicious trap, so is its accuser, and the pot is calling the kettle black.[3]

Many in our century have felt the force of this dilemma. People from all walks of life have exhibited an irrepressible interest in finding meaning which goes beyond the individual. Even atheistic existentialists, who may seem furthest from a search for self-transcending meaning or value, nevertheless exhibit the desire for such meaning. Nietzsche, despite his hostile attitude toward God, moved toward a substitute form of self-transcendence. "Willing the eternal recurrence" was his way of asserting meaning for life. Other convinced atheists like Sartre and Camus yielded to a similar desire and created transcendent meaning by willing or "affirming" the ultimate meaninglessness that their philosophies assert is the basic condition of human existence. In the words of Paul Tillich, each of us has an "ultimate concern"; the desire for absolute meaning in our secular world is not imposed by religion but is an existential reaction against living without a structure of meaning.[4]

The fading confidence in science and naturalism coupled with the natural human desire for ultimate meaning in life have set the stage for the phenomenal growth of interest in a myriad of pantheistic cults and quasi-religions in our culture. The popularity of these various religions can be traced to many causes. First among these is the fact that the pantheistic world view is relatively simple. It stresses an undeniable element of our uni-verse (i.e., unity) and makes this principle the basic concept of its world view. Pantheism also skirts the thorny problem encountered by theism which must explain the presence of evil in a world created and sustained by an omniscient, omnipotent and loving God.

Second, this system assures the pantheist that he is related to ultimate reality. Pantheism's teaching about union with God insures that our hope of self-transcending meaning will be reached. A God who is too disconnected from this world (e.g., a deistic God) lacks the quality of relatedness that is so necessary to religious worship.

Third, pantheism assures its adherents that the reality with which they are in contact is indeed absolute. That is, if "God" designates everything that is, it is obvious that there cannot be anything outside of or more ultimate than "God." Theists have the problem of assuring themselves that the proper God is being worshiped; it is always possible that Allah may be more ultimate than Yahweh. But pantheism, by its all-inclusive nature, automatically solves this polemical problem. No one could possibly accuse the pantheists' God of being less than ultimate.

Fourth, pantheism appears to be the common conclusion of mystics from all ages and cultures who have found union with God in their ecstatic experiences. These esoteric and elite sages seem to have an advantage in "knowing" intuitively the nature of true reality. The mystical route to knowledge seems to be mysterious and transcultural, making its authority hard to deny.

Fifth, perhaps most significantly, the religions that are based on the pantheistic world view commonly minimize the importance of reason, logic and intellectualizing. Instead of a heartless attitude which views people and things in terms of the profit to be made or advantage to be gained, this world view, in the eyes of many, serves to restore the elements of feeling, emotion, intuition and spirituality that an obsessive rationalism precludes. Thus in an overly intellectualistic culture, the pantheistic world view seems to provide an appealing alternative.

Although the pantheistic world view may be gaining popularity in our century, it is by no means new. As C. S. Lewis noted,

Pantheism certainly is . . . congenial to the modern mind; . . . Pantheism is congenial to our minds not because it is the final stage in a slow process of enlightenment, but because it is almost as old as we are. . . . So far from being the final religious refinement, Pantheism is in fact the permanent natural bent of the human mind.[5]

The religious orientation of the ancient Greeks, for example, was often very pantheistic. In the plutonic school which culminated in Plotinus, the pantheistic One beyond being and knowing became the ultimate reality of the universe.

Much of Eastern thought has also exhibited pantheistic overtones. Despite the theistic schools and scriptural passages of some Indian philosophy, the dominant world view of that culture is pantheistic. The metaphysical system that grew in India became the background for many of the major modern religions of the East, including Hinduism and Buddhism.

Alan Watts on Pantheism and Christianity
The world view of Alan Watts, though it represents only one of several types of pantheism, proves an instructive study. Alan Wilson Watts was born on January 15, 1915, in Chislehurst, England, and came to the United States at the age of twenty-three. His interest in Eastern cultures was stirred when as a youngster he read stories about the Chinese detective, Fu Manchu. By the time he was twenty-one, before he left England, he had published *Spirit of Zen*, and his interest

in Buddhism was growing. But he did not consider himself exclusively a Buddhist, for in 1944 he was ordained in Chicago as an Anglican priest. He served from then until 1950 as a spiritual counselor at Northwestern University in Evanston, Illinois.

By August 1950, however, the Anglican priesthood had become a burden to him. Watts felt that the Christian church as a whole was far too dogmatic. He once wrote, for example, that he left the church "not because it doesn't practice what it preaches, but because it preaches." After this period, Watts did attempt one more synthesis between Christianity and pantheism when he wrote *Myth and Ritual in Christianity* in 1953, but he gradually came to feel that this enterprise was doomed because of Christianity's separatist attitude and obsession with logical and theological precision. During the years 1951-57, as this feeling blossomed, Watts taught comparative philosophy at the American Academy of Asian Studies in San Francisco, and from 1956 until his death in 1973 he spent his time writing and lecturing at universities such as Harvard, Yale, Cambridge, Cornell and Chicago.

As an Anglican priest, he wrote *Behold the Spirit* in 1947, arguing that pantheism and Christianity are compatible. *True* Christianity could be found in the writings of the great Christian mystics who experienced "union" with God. According to Watts, the union found in Christianity "is the entirely free, spontaneous and unnecessary gift of the living and loving God," because "the heart of Being is not law and mechanism but life."[6] This distinctive, argued Watts, technically differentiated his view from pantheism, which holds that union with the universe is necessary and determined. Whether this union is necessary or free, Watts felt it to be the clear significance of passages like John 10:30 where Jesus stated, "I and the Father are one."

Watts was influenced in these earlier years by Aldous Huxley who held that all cultures at all times contained individuals who supported the basic pantheistic world view. True

Christianity, for Huxley, was that of Meister Eckhart and St. John of the Cross, not of Augustine, Aquinas, Calvin and Luther. Huxley argued that it made little difference if one were a Buddhist, Hindu or Christian, for all these religions (when properly understood) lead to God. Huxley thus popularized the *Philosophia Perennis*,[7] a combination of the metaphysic that finds a divine reality at the root of this world of objects and persons, the psychology that recognizes in the human psyche something similar to (or identical with) this divine reality and the ethic that finds man's final goal to be the knowledge of this divine ground of being.[8]

A famous Eastern parable illustrates the *Philosophia Perennis* very well. Four men decide to climb a mountain, but they approach it from four different directions. This fact causes no problems for the climbers, however, for all the paths up the mountain eventually lead to the top of the peak. Thus it is with religions: "The Paths are many but their End is One."[9]

At one time Watts argued strongly for a *Philosophia Perennis* which finds its authority corroborated by mystics in vastly differing cultures who brought unique standpoints to their experiences.[10] Later he came to realize that Christianity, as it is traditionally understood, does not agree with this interpretation of the relationship between pantheism and Christianity. Watts wrote in *Beyond Theology* (1964) that his attempt to achieve a synthesis between pantheism and Christianity did not fit the evidence. Christians have not considered their faith to be one of several religions all of which ultimately reach God. Christianity has never lost the element of all-or-nothing commitment to Christ as God's only Son.[11]

It was shortly after publishing *Behold the Spirit* that Watts entered a crucial period in his life. In August 1950 he wrote a lengthy letter to his friends from a farm in Millbrook, New York, to describe his thinking. The "Church's claim to be the best of all ways to God," he said, "is not only a mistake, but also a symptom of anxiety."[12] This letter signaled the end of his tenure as an Anglican priest and foreshadowed a comment in *Beyond Theology* in which he openly admitted that his position was pantheistic: "Any suggestion that there is some inner level at which . . . God and man are identical . . . is dubbed pantheism—as if this anathema simply ended the matter then and there."[13] Later in the book, after expressing his unified view of reality, Watts concluded, "If this is that theological bugbear, pantheism, what of it?"[14]

Watts' version of pantheism is not the absolute monism found in some of the later followers of the eighth-century Hindu philosopher, Śankara. Simple uniformity is a view wherein everything that exists is held to be an undifferentiated whole. In contrast, Watts argued that the world of objects which seems to be made up of opposites must be seen with "correlative vision." We must see that explicit opposites are implicit allies which are related to each other and cannot exist apart. The unity in Watts' pantheism is not "mere oneness as opposed to multiplicity, since these two terms are themselves polar."[15] What we have is not absolute monism, but a pantheism where the principles of One and many are opposed but related, like polar opposites in a single field.

Defining the term *pantheism* often proves difficult. Some assert that words like *monism* and *pantheism* are merely convenient labels used by Western theologians but avoided by the Eastern people themselves. Thus some take offense at the flippant use of these terms.[16] In response, it must be pointed out that we will not use the term *pantheism* pejoratively; we will use the term simply to refer to the general class of religions and metaphysical theories which hold that all levels of reality are related ontologically (that is, with respect to their very being) and ultimately are one. This wide definition includes the view of simple uniformity as well as those views which hold that conceptual opposites (like good evil, God man and body/soul) are opposed but related poles in a single field. Pantheism, then, is the world view which asserts that individual human beings are not ultimately real as separate existents; what exists is, in the final sense, a unified, ontological whole.

A study of Alan Watts' world view is instructive for several reasons. As an eclectic, Watts has pulled together many of the elements common to various Eastern traditions. Thus to critique these common strains in Watts is to evaluate the pantheistic world view in general. Further, as a Westerner Watts has made the thought of Eastern traditions uniquely accessible in the West, and his synthesis of the Orient has achieved a measure of popularity. More important, Watts' personal spiritual odyssey parallels that of many disenchanted Westerners. Just as many an individual (and perhaps the culture as a whole) has moved away from complete confidence in human reason to a more intuitive approach to reality, so Watts in his personal life abandoned what he considered a rationalistic Christianity in favor of a world view which finally eliminates conceptual thought. For these reasons Alan Watts provides an excellent opportunity to discuss the general world view of pantheism and to examine its implications for daily living.

2

WATTS
PANTHEISTIC
SYSTEM

Many writers have admonished Westerners to be cautious about putting Eastern ways of thinking into Western molds. Eastern thought must be understood on its own grounds, argue these writers. Any attempt to squeeze it into Western categories is doomed to failure.[1] And so the world view of Alan Watts finds ultimate reality to be beyond the conceptual distinctions that characterize much of Western philosophy.

Many Westerners think that the logical rules of thought (such as the principle that a statement and its logical opposite cannot both be true in the same sense at the same time) actually apply to reality. But a few Westerners, like the neoplatonist Plotinus who has already been mentioned, think that what is ultimately real does not conform to or is not limited by such rules of thought. Reality is actually outside the realm governed by the rules of thought based on opposing concepts such as up/down, transcendent/immanent or secular/sacred. In contrast to most Westerners, Watts agrees with Plotinus on this point. "Being beyond duality" forms the basic premise of Watts' world view.[2]

Being beyond Duality

Watts acknowledges that reality as we perceive it does not appear to be unified into one ontological whole. Knowledge which comes through the senses involves a relationship between knower and known which would contradict an absolute monism. Factual description (including science) depends on an independent and detached observer. But according to Watts, this feeling of contrast between subject and object is merely conventional, although it serves a useful purpose within certain limits. The problem has been that Westerners have ignored a fact which slips through the "net of factual language": no independent observer really exists as an individual.[3]

The fact that we perceive opposites through our senses does not discount the fact, according to Watts, that all duality presupposes a unity. We can discover by means of a "secret path" that "Hell implies Heaven, and Satan implies the Lord." While some pantheists go so far as to say that black is the same as white, Watts holds a softer view wherein contrasting facets of reality are bound up in a higher unification.[4]

The Polar Nature of Reality. Watts describes the universe as a polar entity. In this view, polarity means something more than mere duality or opposition. To hold two aspects of reality to be polar is to see their intrinsic and basic relationship; "they are the terms, ends, or extremities of a single whole." Like the poles of the earth, the two ends of a magnet or the two faces of a coin, polar opposites are inseparable opposites. The polar opposites are abstractions brought about by the mind's conceptualizing process, and thus the conceptual extremes have a less "substantial" existence than the undivided reality which lies between the poles.[5]

This polar view of reality is reflected in the ancient Eastern concept of Yin Yang. This principle is often depicted by the symbol of two idealized fish, one black and one white, which are swimming together to form a perfect circle. Each fish has its head in the other's tail, so that they mutually form a circular whole as they swim eternally in a ring. This famous symbol illustrates the principle that each aspect of reality, like those two fish, depends on the other aspects of reality for its own existence.[6]

The Field behind Duality. Convention makes the universe seem ultimately bifurcated. But because the dualities that ultimately comprise reality are correlative and interacting, this universe cannot be fully understood through a subject/object type of knowledge. Instead, both aspects of the duality must be taken into account for ultimate truth transcends every conceptualization to become undifferentiated Wisdom. The realization of a "field" behind the dichotomies of conventional learning and knowing is necessary for the mind to be free of the fiction of an independent observer.[7]

The being (as well as the knowing) of all organisms, like the Yin Yang fish, depends on the environment in which it exists. No thing or organism exists or acts on its own. Each is an aspect of the entire process going on around it. Just as an individual cell in the human heart depends on the whole heart, so the heart itself depends on the whole body. The body, in turn, depends on the community of human beings in the same way, and the whole community depends on its entire environment. The aspects of this universe are not like pieces of a jigsaw puzzle each of which has separate existence, for our world is really a complex wiggliness, devoid of individual parts.[8] Every organism is a process which can only be understood in relation to the larger and longer movement of its environment.

The process of unifying simpler (apparently opposite) components into a larger unit can go on until all reality has become a unified whole. Watts does precisely this. In the final analysis, *God* designates the Being beyond duality. The ultimate is "God as he is absolutely in himself, beyond all duality—neither one nor many, nor both one and many, and yet with equal reality one and many."[9]

Such language (which Watts admits makes little sense

from a dualistic standpoint) might seem to point toward a sort of ethereal state of consciousness as ultimate reality. But Watts rejects this conclusion because the physical world does not vanish into an undifferentiated or bodiless luminescence. Rather, Watts sees all physical distinctions as obvious expressions of unity. As Chinese painting so clearly illustrates, an individual tree or mountain is not *on* but *with* the space that forms the background.[10] In fact, argues Watts, this polar/field view of reality may be gaining recognition in modern scientific thinking. Despite the erroneous presupposition of science (i.e., that independent observers exist), science is beginning to recognize that causally connected things are not really separate and that the causal principle is a "fumbling way of recognizing that cause A and effect B go together in the same way as the head and tail of a cat." Science now thinks in terms of fields, whether magnetic, spatial or social. Detailed descriptions are now commonly made in terms of organism/environment or figure/ground.[11]

The Idealistic Nature of Reality. Fundamentally, Watts' view of reality is an idealism, a view of reality which says that whatever exists is essentially spiritual or mental in composition. He held that sensation is the result of some vibration interacting with a mind. Without mind our world is "devoid of light, heat, weight, solidity, motion, space, time, or any other imaginable feature." The vibrations with which mind interacts are like the sound of one hand clapping or like the sticks beating a skinless drum, to use ancient Eastern illustrations. Just as no light beams are visible in space until reflected off minute specks of dust, so the vibrations of sound or light do not actually become sound or light until they interact with the eye or ear of a living organism.[12]

Because reality is idealistic, the dualistic concepts of human minds can be applied to reality only when this interaction takes place. Duality arises only when concrete reality is confused with the abstract categories of our conventional way of thinking. For Watts, the figure/ground image which implies mutuality of organism and environment conforms to reality more closely than our exclusive conceptual interpretations. These distinctions (e.g., the contrast between good and evil) are not truly descriptive of ultimate reality.[13]

This emphasis on the idealistic nature of reality strongly influences Watts' concept of God as a personal Being. No longer is God outside the world sovereignly guiding the universe. For Watts, this view fosters false security, for the God/world distinction, like all other conceptualizations, is less than real. In the end, "the thing-in-itself (Kant's *ding an sich*), whether animal, vegetable or mineral, is not only unknowable—it does not exist."[14]

Universal Support for This System. This world view may sound strange to one who is not familiar with it. But Watts argues, "The fact of a given union with God, given without respect to virtue or holiness, has been the central and secret joy of many a great mystic, Christian and non-Christian, in all times and cultures."[15] The deepest mystical and spiritual insights of many ages and cultures form the authority for this world view.

While the highest authority does come from intuitive experience, Watts also argues that the Christian Scripture provides secondary support for his polar/field view of reality whenever it testifies to an insight of oneness on the part of a biblical author. This is the significance of John 10:30: "I and the Father are one." Isaiah's words, "That men may know, from the rising of the sun and from the west, that there is none beside me; I am the LORD, and there is no other" (Is. 45:6), express the divinity of everything that exists. When the apostle Paul stated that we are to be "in Christ" or "to be partakers of his flesh and blood," he meant that we should recognize, as did Jesus, our fundamental identity with him who is "I Am" before Abraham was.[16] For Watts, even the Bible hints that ultimate reality is composed of ontologically related poles which exist in a single field.

Maya: The World of Illusion

According to some ancient Hindu schools of thought, our world is *maya*. This concept has been defined in many ways and has caused much confusion. Even today there is little unanimity in definition. Śankara, the greatest of the Vedantists, found absolute monism distasteful, for the reality of the world of objects and persons strongly impressed his consciousness. He therefore employed the concept *maya* to mean something which, although less than real, nevertheless strongly impressed one as being real. Watts defines *maya* as "magical illusion," meaning that this universe is an exciting, electrical or interesting illusion. He wanted to add the idea that *maya* is not the terrified fear of the unknown. For Watts, *maya* connotes the fascinating illusion of a magic show.[17]

Creation. The world as part of the universe was created by the One Being beyond duality. According to Watts, the Genesis account clearly shows that God was not working according to a preconceived plan. Creation was spontaneous; every successive stage completely surprised him so that only after God completed the process could he declare, "Behold it is very good!" God frivolously created platypuses and whales (oops!), and when he had completed that he took the clay figurine of Adam (made in his image) and breathed himself into Adam's nostrils. The *ruach adonai*, the same Spirit of God that first moved on the face of the waters, came to inhabit the image of clay. But when the Lord looked out through the eyes of the figurine, he forgot who he was. From that moment on, the Lord's alter egos began to conjure up the image of an Old Gentleman, white beard, robe and all, as a person other than themselves. Thus we forgot that this whole world is a charade.[18]

In contrast to the theistic God who freely willed the creation, creation for Watts occurred when God "othered" himself. We do not enter an existing world, "we come *out* of it, as leaves from a tree." Just as the ocean "waves" and a bud "flowers," the universe "peoples." Thus each individual is an expression of the whole of nature; each person is the unique action of the whole universe.[19]

These metaphors are familiar in the general pantheistic world view. Creation for a pantheist is generally emanational in nature, which means that the world comes out of God. For Watts, creation out of nothing is actually creation out of *sunyata* (a Zen concept literally meaning "no-thing," but including the ideas of creative possibilities and potentials). Watts takes *sunyata* to be the "unutterable mystery, the divine darkness, which is God himself."[20] Creation, then, arises not from the free choice of a sovereign God but from a spontaneous emanation out of God's own being.

The Chess Game. If this world was created out of God so that humans are really one unified person, how is it that interpersonal relationships seem so real? Watts' basic answer is implicit in the concept of *maya* as a trick or magical illusion in the positive sense. In the case of genuine conflict the lines between the two sides are drawn with seriousness. But when this universe exhibits interaction, the confrontation is like a friendly chess game not an international war. In the friendly game there will always be a tacit understanding between the two sides, at least until one of the two players becomes upset with the proceedings. If that should happen, the game comes to an end. The universe approximates the chess game where God and the alter ego are the two players. Concludes Watts: "I can play chess with myself to the degree that, when I am playing the white side, I can pretend that I am not the same person who plays the black. And so plays the universe."[21]

Before the Lord began functioning in this new world, a conference was held with Satan, and the primordial conspiracy (spoken of in the book of Job) was plotted. To understand this fact is to look at our universe realistically, but it also has some drawbacks, even for Watts. To see through the game requires somewhat more bravado than playing it seriously. To take seriously the stakes of heaven and hell involves little risk. But seeing through the primordial conspiracy is dan gerous for it entails the awful blasphemy of saying that the Lord and the Devil might really be one.[22]

If this world is not ultimately serious, then there must be some way to discover that fact. How can we see through the charade? Watts answers that there are "cues," much like proscenium arches in theaters, which suggest to us that the world order is but a drama. For example, there is the ambivalence of the carnival and the holiday. The lawful fasting of Lent contrasts with the gaity and license of the Mardi gras. The unique institutions of the Sabbath, when God rested from creating, and the Year of Jubilee, when all debts were canceled, act like cracks in the wall which enable us to see through to the fact that we are playing a cosmic game of chess and that occasionally the rules of this game can be suspended.

If the social order can be completely upset (as in Jubilee) and the moral system which we usually follow can be set aside on occasion without disastrous consequences (as in Mardi gras), then these principles which order our lives must be less than absolute. That they can be safely ignored at certain times suggests that they are but conventional rules which have no basis in reality. These hints cue us, as does the frame of a picture, to recognize that what we are perceiving may not be ultimately real.[23]

This discussion immediately raises questions concerning the meaning of ethical norms. If Mardi gras can arbitrarily suspend the rules every February, then is there any ultimate sense in which they must be followed the rest of the year? Indeed what are the merits of differing versions of this cosmic game, for example, the bee-game, the ant-game or the human-game? Is one more valuable than another? For Watts, these variations of the game only elaborate the proverb, "Variety is the spice of life." In a real sense, the universe "othering" itself is not a free and thus significant event. In the case of human society, the guidelines of religion and ethics are only the optimal rules for the game; other guidelines are easily possible.[24]

The Nature and Place of Evil. This view of our universe generates other questions. The human experience of moral evil seems to be a problem for a world view which asserts that the Lord is playing a game of chess. But for Watts, good/ evil is like up/down: both are abstract categories which cannot perform their function unless they are kept strictly apart. But neither of these categorical distinctions really describes the way things are.[25] In a moral sense, the good/evil distinction merits no real status, since it exists only on the conceptual level.

Having eliminated traditional moral values, Watts asserts that psychological difficulties are likewise pseudoproblems. The trouble with the individual who may be suffering from what we call psychosis or neurosis lies with society as a whole: the convention of the separate individual ego foisted upon human consciousness by generations of habit accounts for mental disorders. Psychological problems are not the malfunction of this ego or that ego but are a result of the ego-illusion in general. The solution involves seeing the proscenium arches. If the mind could discover that, as a solitary ego, it faces a world it falsely considers alien and foreign, and if we could see that our universe is really a friendly environment, then psychological problems would be eliminated.[26]

Physical pain is dealt with in a similar fashion. As is often the case with idealism, physical pain is a "hypnotic state" which can be switched on or off at will.[27] However unsatisfying this conclusion may be to the suffering cancer patient, it is nevertheless the logical outworking of this idealistic world view.

But the pseudofeelings of suffering do perform a valuable function. The agony of physical pain can act to explode the shell in which our individual egos have become solidly encased. Physical suffering can become the nutcracker which gets inside the shell of individuality which has been built up for (false) security around the isolated ego. Somehow, if one becomes loosened from the tightening grip of individual personality, a true view of reality will result.[28]

The Ego-Illusion

Much of what has already been said implies that the individual ego, as we are accustomed to experiencing it, is not a real entity. According to Watts, when the Lord set up the primordial chess game, he forgot that the black side is actually the alter ego. He forgot that the two fish that swim eternally in a circle are really two aspects of one reality. But it seems undeniable that our consciousness receives a constant bombardment of sensations which seem to confirm our individual existence. If this constant stream of consciousness seems forcefully to support an idea that is contrary to reality, it seems necessary to account for these illusory sensations. Watts tries to do just that.

The Cause of the Ego-Illusion. Buddhism teaches that we suffer because of our craving for objects which are essentially impermanent. One of the strongest desires humans have is for a personal existence. The isolated ego originated as a mental castle into which one of the original chess players retreated in order to protect (and make permanent) its own existence. This castle then provided a starting point from which the ego could resist change, shut out suffering and build a personal existence. In this way the ego seemed to achieve a measure of control over its own destiny and happiness. In short, this castle became the means for the individual to resist life.[29]

This way of thinking, erroneous though it is, became solidified by centuries of convention. Psychological prejudice and semantic confusion have through the ages made it common sense to think that the patterns, shapes and structures of our world are forms *of* something. According to Watts, these objects remain as dispensable as the tortoise on which the world was once supposed to stand.[30]

The rediscovery of original unity came through the experiments of the Chinese and Indian mystics who intuited a sense of continuity between the depths of humanity (*atman*) and the depths of the universe (*Brahman*). But since ancient times the theistic religions of the West have resisted this Eastern insight because their dependence on revelation as the source of all religious truth petrified the ego-illusion.

According to Watts, Protestantism and Catholicism have worked in alliance to intensify the individual's feelings of separation. The Roman Catholic Church brings God very close in the sacraments but holds him away by the very intensity of worship and adoration. Protestantism inculcates a permanent sense of guilt which fosters an atmosphere of spiritual gloom as one grovels before the Righteous Judge.[31] The biblical view of the universe is based, for the most part, on an analogy between nature and the ancient Oriental governments with their terrible monarchs and their bowing and scraping subjects. But, he continues, the world view which best suits the empirical climate of the twentieth century is the one based on the unitive experiences of the Eastern mystics.[32]

Results of the Ego-Illusion. The individual ego creates a heightened sense of anxiety. Our way of thinking has divided our unified experience into separated facts in order to facilitate our observation of individual events. But this inculcates a sense of guilt and responsibility, for as individual egos we can no longer depend on instinct or spontaneity for direction. Rather than enjoying the comfort of sitting back to let events and processes move fluidly along, we begin to feel as though we are ultimately responsible. The result of our retreat into an ego-castle has been the opposite of what we had hoped for.[33]

The convention of individual egos has bound our society into ethical paralysis. Despite the best intentions of those who would avoid the ego-illusion, the escape attempt always involves self-defeating activity. The moment one becomes seriously involved in avoiding the ego-illusion, one excludes some other group which seeks to escape the problem by another means. The experience reminds one of infancy when everyone says that you *must* be free, responsible and loving; you become "helplessly defined as an independent agent."[34] The ethical double-bind which results from the command, "Thou shalt *love* . . . ," becomes at once a problem which results from the ego-illusion and a hint (like the picture frame) that the ego is in fact an illusion.

This illusion puts us in a hostile relationship with our environment. We must view the world "outside" through the little windows in the towers of our ego-castle. Thus Westerners are perpetually conquering nature, space, bacteria and insects instead of cooperating with them to achieve harmony.[35] If indeed we are poles within a field, vitally related to our environment, we should have an entirely different view of both ecology and sociology. What Western societies need to see is that this "world is all of a piece like the head-tailed cat."[36]

Advantages of Eliminating the Illusion. Watts clearly argues that the ego-illusion had best be eliminated. According to him, those who insist on the supreme value of the individual (and thus the desirability of immortality) have not given their position careful thought. As the borough of Manhattan has found, building higher and higher is valuable only to a point: above a certain height the gains in floor space are outweighed by the large amount of space taken up by girders and elevators on lower floors. Concludes Watts, the "indefinite prolongation of the individual is bad design—architecturally, biologically, and psychologically."[37]

Of course the primary reason for eliminating this persistent ego-illusion is to discover what is actually true about reality. Though it is a feeling experienced by almost everyone, the sensation of being lonely and temporary visitors in the universe is, according to Watts, in "flat contradiction" to everything we know about humanity and our environment via the physical sciences.[38] Leaving aside the question of why Watts appeals to science, it seems that he believes this view is "true" and that we ought to believe it.

One of the advantages of eliminating the ego-illusion revolves around a new concept of death. If death is a serious event which happens to real individuals, forcing them to face a genuine heaven/hell situation, then there can be no doubt that it is a terrifying concept. However, the "constrictions and spasms" of death are a frightful agony only if one is persuaded that individuals live in this universe once and only once, and that this life contains moral compulsions and duties. But to see that our individual existence is illusory is to take a healthy new view of death which could go a long way toward alleviating the anxiety of modern life.[39]

The eternal Self of the universe is constantly going through the cycle of death and rebirth. This process has the advantage of relieving the tedium of immortality, thus easing the boredom that would set in if things were to stay the same eternally. Physical death, therefore, is a means of eternal renewal. It provides food for other organisms, but more importantly it wipes away the memory, which, if it were to accumulate indefinitely, would "strangle all creative life with a sense of unutterable monotony." Death ends the memory system called "me" but it does not end the eternal Self, the real Me. Thus the world of reality is, according to Watts, ever present and always new, without the cumbersome baggage of a past.[40]

Probably the most immediate result of this new understanding of reality is the psychological feeling of relief. When one finally realizes that mind and body are one, that the patterns, forms and structures of reality as we perceive them are dispensable, an awakening of tremendous proportions occurs. The bag of skin we call a "body" is part of the ego-illusion, and when we rid ourselves of this, we will experience a curiously exhilarating liberation.[41] If life on planet Earth is not serious after all, then we can sit back without pressure and enjoy.

Summary

Several summary comments will serve to conclude our discussion of Watts' world view. First, for Watts, mystics have intuited both the unity of the universe on the one hand and the polar nature of many aspects of the universe on the other. Without this polar view of reality, the principle of plurality would contrast God as something outside his unity, and reality would be dualistic at its highest level.[42] Thus in contrast to strict monism, Watts' pantheism includes both the principles of unity and plurality within the ultimate unity of God. In the words of Radhakrishnan, God also contains a transcendent aspect. This world is in God, but it does not exhaust him. God as ultimate reality unifies all polar opposites (like unity and plurality, transcendence and immanence) into a single field.[43]

Second, for Watts and pantheism in general, the creation of God is an emanational and spontaneous unfolding of God's being. Just as the oceans "wave," so the universe "peoples." The necessity of creation is stronger for some other pantheistic thinkers than it is for Watts. His concept is closer to an unpremeditated, perfectly spontaneous unfolding. But this amounts to saying nearly the same thing, for the creation of Watts' God catches him completely by surprise. Unlike the creation by Yahweh, who spoke with authority out of premeditated freedom, creation in pantheism occurs spontaneously by chance.[44]

Third, pantheism for the most part does not assert that the world of sensation is totally illusory. The world of multiplicity enjoys a place as one of the poles of God, for if the all-inclusiveness of God did not include multiplicity, then there would be something outside and above God. God's ultimate unity therefore includes facets of both unity and multiplicity. But one should not conclude from this that the world as we perceive it is ultimately real. This world of sensation and duality cannot be taken with final seriousness. There are certain hints (like picture frames and proscenium arches) which have been picked up by mystics of all ages. These cue us that this world order is a drama and ought to be understood in light of the primordial conspiracy. Thus while the world exists as part of God, it does not exist on its own as an entity or series of entities in any ultimate sense.[45]

Fourth, the reality status of human beings is similar to that of the world order. Persons are not totally illusory, for they constitute one pole of God. Persons are important aspects of the universe, forming part of the field for others around them. But in the ultimate sense, persons *as individuals* do not exist. "Humanity is not one thing and the world another; . . . any organism is so embedded in its environment that the evolution of so complex and intelligent a creature as man could never have come to pass without a reciprocal evolution of the environment."[46] As for our normal modes of thinking, factual description depends on the convention that there can be a detached observer to regard the world objectively. In the final analysis, however, no independent observer exists.[47]

In sum, the universe is a unified field in which opposing poles are brought together so that the many is in the One and not the One in the many. The universe (God) did not freely create but spontaneously generated a world which is less than ultimately real as we conventionally perceive it. Our sensations and thoughts express to us a serious situation wherein human beings are faced with real life and death alternatives. But since our individual ego depends on a fiction, we must realize that the world is only a cosmic drama with which we ought to play along. In the final analysis, this drama, with its conventional rules and ethical guidelines, is of no ultimate significance since all polar particulars adhere in the One unified God who is the universe.

3

WATTS ON CHRISTIANITY

Alan Watts' view of Christianity and its relation to other religions, especially those holding a pantheistic view of reality, changed over the course of his life. How this change took place makes an interesting study.

The Philosophia Perennis

Watts has argued that mystics from all ages and all cultures have intuited his basic view of reality. Aldous Huxley took the common threads of the various schools of mysticism and popularized the notion that these schools all experienced the same reality. He borrowed (from the German philosopher Leibniz) the term *Philosophia Perennis* (the "Perennial Philosophy") to designate the common world view of these various groups of thinkers. This theory raises the question as to how religions with very diverse doctrines can all mean the same thing. To solve this problem, an important distinction was made.

Form vs. Meaning. According to Watts, most people, including clergy and theologians, confuse the "meaning" of religion with the "form" of religion. But an important contrast must be drawn between these two notions if the *Philosophia Perennis* is to be maintained. The form of religion, on the one hand, concerns certain doctrines and precepts usually based primarily on historical events. Form therefore varies from one religion to the next depending on the historical basis of the particular religion. On the other hand, the meaning of all religions is God himself, the ultimate as an experienced reality. Meaning is common to all religions: it is the apprehension of the state of consciousness that the apostle Paul called "the mind of Christ." Though incapable of exact description, meaning may be explained so as to give traditional forms much more clarity than they now possess.[1]

The historical grounding of religious forms necessarily makes them impermanent; by their very nature they tend to die. Thus spiritual growth sometimes depends on relinquishing specific forms. But this does not mean that forms are insignificant, for their transience is their very.life. Thus forms serve significantly as impermanent, changing expressions of eternal meaning, but without that meaning the forms are useless.[2]

The main insight of the *Philosophia Perennis* is that meaning remains constant from one religion to the next regardless of historical form. For this reason Huxley could espouse the Eastern illustration of the four climbers who took four different paths up the mountain. In the end they all reached the top.

The Content of the Philosophia Perennis. Huxley distilled three basic areas of common meaning from the writings of the mystics. The most basic of these is the metaphysical unity of reality which recognizes that the world is substantially unified. The second of these concerns the areas of anthropology and psychology. Huxley held that the human soul is somehow identical with divine reality. The third of these lies in the area of ethics. The *Philosophia Perennis* takes ethical injunctions to mean the gaining of knowledge about our ultimate unity with the immanent and transcendent Ground of being.[3] Ultimately there are no rules governing the actions of one person toward another, for there are no persons to do the acting; there is only One Ego.

The Chinese Box. If this view of metaphysical reality, anthropology and ethical imperatives comprises the true way of looking at things, it would seem that orthodox Christianity is wrong and ought to be abandoned. However, such a move would go against the confessed thesis of the Philosophia Perennis: all religions contain essentially the same meaning. According to this view, the forms of religion which differ because of their divergent historical origins should be recognized for their ultimate inadequacy. By apprehending the meaning behind the forms, these forms may become intelligible to the modern mind and exhibit the power to move the soul as they should.[4]

However, the meaning of the dogmas of various religions does not become self-evident by mere juxtaposition. They must be woven into some sort of organic relationship if the common thread of meaning is to become clear. Watts enlists a "contextual" method for this enterprise. Known as the "Chinese box," this method fits one religion into another, without changing the positive assertions of either religion. For example, the Hebrew Scriptures were included in the Christian Bible, and while Jewish believers may feel as though violence has been done, nothing which is positively asserted about God and humanity in Judaism must be excluded from Christianity. On the other side of the coin there are many positive assertions of Christianity which do not fit the traditional Jewish view of our relationship to God.[5] Thus Watts could argue that if Judaism were true, Christianity could not be true. But if Christianity were true, Judaism could also be true and none of its major doctrines would need be sacrificed.

Just as the Chinese box worked for Christianity to actively incorporate the Jewish view of reality, so the Hindu world view can swallow the Christian doctrines. While such reasoning may not please the orthodox Christian, neither did the Christian use of the Old Testament put Jewish adherents in the best of spirits. Therefore, if Christianity is true, Hinduism cannot be true, because Christianity emphasizes the transcendence of God to the exclusion of his immanence. But if Hinduism is true, Christianity can also be true, for Hinduism maintains God's transcendence as one of the very important poles of reality.[6]

Watts held, in accordance with the *Philosophia Perennis*, that all forms of religion were historical expressions of a single, unified meaning. He once argued "that which has been held 'everywhere, always, and by all' is the one common realization, doctrine, and myth which has appeared with consistent unanimity in every culture, without benefit of 'historical contacts' between the various traditions."[7] For Watts, herein lies the significance of the virgin-born One who is both God and man. Jesus, like every person, is an incarnation (what the Hindus call an *avatar*) of the "only begotten Son" and thus expresses meaning on behalf of the One and only Self, Yahweh, I Am.[8]

The Early Watts on the Incarnation

In his early writings, Watts clearly thought Christianity to be one of the many forms that expresses one eternal meaning. As an Anglican priest he argued that this universe was unified at its highest level, but it was necessary for him to support this contention, for it seems to contradict the traditional beliefs of Christianity. Watts therefore argued that the earliest Christians believed in the unadulterated unity of this universe, but that several important influences caused later Christian thinkers to ignore the original insights of their own tradition.

Roots of the Present Spiritual Condition. Despite the fact that the monotheistic religions of Judaism and Christianity are in theory opposed to dualism, a world view which posits two eternal and opposing beings or forces, they were profoundly influenced by Zoroastrianism. Watts argued that Zoroastrian dualism provided the impetus for Judaism to assert itself as an ethical monotheism. But with the absolutizing of the principle of good, according to Watts, Judaism was forced to confer the same status on the evil principle. In ethical monotheism, evil becomes an effective and thus highly dangerous rebellion against the Creator. The energy with which evil is opposed by theists shows they acknowledge a devil with almost godlike power. The greater the ethical ideal, the darker is the shadow that it casts. Thus Judeo-Christian ethical monotheism became, according to Watts, at least in attitude, the world's greatest dualism.[9]

Christians then began to look down on the one aspect of this dualism. Once the devil became a real person in the minds of Christians, he and God were abstracted into the sphere of real external objects. It soon followed that the eternal reality of individual ego-souls became desirable and necessary. Subsequently, the ego-soul was connected to a body which had to be stripped away if the individual was to find an eternal relationship with the Lord and avoid the devil. According to Watts' analysis, there arose a distaste for the flesh, despite the fact that "the Word was made Flesh" and "God so loved the world."[10]

Christianity in turn influenced all of Western culture. Because Eastern societies maintained a closer relationship with unified reality than have their Western counterparts, they have exhibited more stability and significance. Our civilization, however, is in the process of disintegration because the pervasive influence of Christianity has stunted the growth of the principle of unity.

Christianity, the source of the problem in Watts' opinion, has done nothing to alleviate it. It has in fact accentuated the sense of distinction between God and humanity—Catholicism by the very intensity of worship and Protestantism by its insistence on harsh, unachievable ethical demands. The modern churches are too concerned with nonessentials (e.g., witnessing, praying or preaching) to accomplish the major task: giving deluded individuals a consciousness of union with God. In a word, concludes Watts, because Christianity is not a mystical religion, it is not fully and essentially religious.[11]

The churches have failed so miserably in their task of presenting the world with a basic consciousness of unity that religion in the churches has been reduced to mimicry. Theologians grasp the forms of religion with great precision and clarity. But in the practice of religion, they merely imitate the actions of the mystical saints, forever misunderstanding the power behind those actions. They become like monkeys, trying to gain consciousness of the saints' religion by copying their actions and ideas. But because the meaning behind the activity escapes them, the task reduces to an unproductive drudgery. The more futile the attempt becomes, the harder they try, but they always seem to fall short, attributing the fact that they fail to not imitating hard enough. Concludes Watts, the whole process becomes a vicious circle of futility.[12]

The Development of Christianity. Despite the shortcomings of today's churches, true Christianity began with the unique consciousness of Oneness that characterizes true religion. As any informed student of the history and psychology of religion will know, argues Watts, Christ himself had an intense experience of "cosmic consciousness," that mystical, intuitive experience of unity with God. He experienced the realization that each of us is a manifestation of the Bible's "I Am." This consciousness of unity with God is what caused Christ's crucifixion, for in a culture where Yahweh was considered radically transcendent, experiencing "cosmic consciousness" was tantamount to blasphemy. In India, however, where the people understand this sort of experience, everyone would have laughed and rejoiced with Christ. Hindus understand that "we are all God in disguise—playing hide-and-seek with himself."[13]

From those early years of Christianity, the religion has grown along predictable lines. There was the childhood of the medieval times when wisdom was accepted on authority in a naive, literal and external way. This childhood stage emphasized God the Father, often bordering on a heresy called monophysitism. Next came the period of adolescence with its rebellious questioning of authority. The Protestant Reformation initiated this stage, and the second person of the Trinity became the most significant of the Godhead. Then came the movement away from religion and the adult stage found Western culture increasingly interested in materialism and imperial growth. Secularism became a brief pause between stages of religious development. But in Watts' analysis, we are now moving into the mature stage where the wisdom on which the culture was originally founded will again be emphasized. This mature stage, though it may lack the physical strength of youth, will not lack for spiritual strength and maturity.

The mature stage, wherein the Holy Spirit will emerge as the most important person of the Trinity, will emphasize three facets of insight in its approach to daily life. One of these will be the given union of the soul with God. Since God is merciful and forgiving, he has already accepted us with all our sins and imperfections. Another of these will be the emphasis on love as the instrument of combat with evil instead of the hatred and violence common in brash, youthful stages. The last of these will find morality motivated by gratitude for the gift of union with God and not by a neurotic sense of guilt and obedience to law and authority.[14]

Proper Understanding of Christianity. When maturity in Christianity has been reached, argues Watts, we will begin to understand the original meaning of Christian doctrines or forms. Creation *ex nihilo* (out of nothing) is a good example of orthodox Christianity's misinterpretation, for Christians literally and naively accepted the expression of the doctrine while ignoring its meaning. According to Watts, the "nothing" of creation *ex nihilo* really means "no-thing," or in Eastern terms *sunyata*, which refers really to "the unutterable mystery, the divine darkness, which is God himself." Watts argues that the apparent Void is really God as he is in himself (beyond all duality), not God as he appears to us in the necessarily dualistic modes of speech and thought.[15]

The true significance of the Incarnation can be seen in this light. The meaning of Christ's existence is the transformation of humanity into God. The divine nature in humans must awaken, so that they will understand their true Selfhood. Theological Christianity has admitted that Christ is an example of God and man united, but mythological Christianity retains the insight that Christ was not a historical abnormality. The Incarnation is unique, not in that it involves only one individual, but in that "it is the only real event, the only occurrence which is *now*, which is not past and abstract."[16] The process of incarnation, which is the process of uniting God and humanity, only began in Jesus. Now it must extend from him to include the whole universe.[17]

The Lord's Supper likewise originally conveyed the same significance as did the Incarnation. Its real meaning is that when we eat, the elements become part of our body, making our body Christ's. Therefore, the Eucharist should never be mere symbol, for the bread and wine must actually (not figuratively) become the very Christ. In this, the almost magical character of the Catholic Mass, the whole truth lies. Attempts to rationalize or symbolize the Lord's Supper deprive it of its real meaning.[18] The phrase "in remembrance of me" thus recalls "the unity which exists before the apparent scattering or breaking of the One into the Many, before the entrancement of the Lord in his *maya*."[19]

Worship also takes on a new significance. No longer should churches be the "finger-wagging, Bible-banging, breast-thumping, floor-licking" type, where parishioners come to worship out of a sense of duty. Rather Watts envisions a "Church of All Fools," where worshipers laugh like

Dante's angels because they have just seen through "the enormous trick that the Lord has played on himself in pretending to be us—scaring the Living Daylight out of himself by acting the lonely ego tormented by sin, with death and hell at last."[20] Worship here is spontaneous, for staying in bed or taking a swim is better than worship done strictly out of duty. Worship should be a "celestial whoopee," consisting "not of rousing gospel hymns and hearty handshakes at the door" but of the worshipers' true insight into the unified nature of the universe.[21]

The concept of conversion undergoes some scrutiny as well. According to Watts, there are several similarities between sudden conversion within Christianity and the Zen Buddhist experience known as *satori*.[22] The major goal of both types of conversion is not remission from sins before a just God but seeing through the crack in the wall of existence. Suddenly seeing, in that ineffable, mystical experience, that all life is on a stage surrounded by that ever present arch, gives us a whole new outlook on life. In this experience, the sense of separate individuality and conscious will power is carried to an absurd extreme, at which point the ego-illusion "explodes into the discovery of our original and eternal Identity." At the moment of conversion our adventure into separate personality comes to a screeching halt just as it began, namely, by God's *kenosis* or self-emptying. The ego-illusion which began when God poured his spirit, the *ruach adonai*, into Adam ends when we realize that we are really God, the Self of the universe, eternally losing himself, and then finding himself again whenever the ego-illusion is exploded in *satori*.[23]

The Later Watts on Christianity
Watts' earlier writings followed Huxley's thesis and saw Christianity as one of many forms, all of which express the same meaning. But later, Watts began to realize that Christianity (as it is traditionally understood) is simply incompati-

ble with a metaphysical position which places its primary emphasis on the unity of all reality. Accordingly there can be seen in Watts' writings a shift toward the view that one cannot be a pantheist and an orthodox Christian at the same time.

The Shift in Watts' Thinking. The most overt expression of a change in Watts' view comes in the preface of his 1964 book, *Beyond Theology*. Here he notes that his three major attempts at a synthesis between traditional Christianity and the unitive mysticism of the East have failed to take into account the facet of Christianity which is "uncompromising, ornery, militant, rigorous, imperious, and invincibly self-righteous." The earlier books (*Behold the Spirit*, 1947; *The Supreme Identity*, 1950; and *Myth and Ritual in Christianity*, 1953) did not fully recognize Christianity's basic distaste for the idea of a *Philosophia Perennis*. [24]

From right-wing Catholics to left-wing, existential Protestants, Christianity requires a total commitment to Jesus as the unique Incarnation of God. Watts' early attempts at a synthesis ignored the Christian insistence on a real contrast between Creator and creature. [25] The fact that Christianity claims to be ultimately true about the way things are cannot be denied, nor can the corollary of this claim that other religions are less true. Watts finally agreed.

Watts was coming to the point where he realized that a decision had to be made between Christianity and the unitive insights of Eastern philosophy. Even before his repudiation of Christianity he wrote in that climactic letter of August 1950 from the Millbrook farm in New York that he had been questioning the relative truths of the spiritual teachings of the Orient and the doctrines of Christianity for some time. Finally he decided that the church's claim to Truth (a claim, according to Watts, often insisted on by Christians in total ignorance of other revelations) demonstrated a certain inferiority complex. Though it took him some time to reach this decision, he wrote unequivocally in that letter, "I am now fully persuaded that the Church's claim to be the best of all ways to God is not only a mistake, but also a symptom of anxiety."[26] He was later to write that claims to Truth are boorish and inept; he recognized that Christianity and pantheism are not compatible world views, the Chinese box notwithstanding.[27]

Watts Rejects Orthodox Christianity. The basic criticism of traditional Christianity, according to Watts' later writings, is the monarchial imagery used to express the status of God in relation to humanity. Christianity tends to think of God in terms of a patriarch or king, but this thinking arose out of illusory models, myths and language systems which have always been used to make sense out of the world. These images, developed by people who were ruled by Oriental monarchs, have an almost hypnotic effect on human perceptions. The apparently insoluble problem of evil in a universe created and sustained by an omnipotent and omniscient God is really a pseudoproblem which arises from the model itself.[28] For Watts, it became impossible to think of God as having the monarchial and paternal character of Yahweh as he is presented in the Bible.[29]

Watts pronounces orthodox Christianity guilty of corrupting the religion *of* Jesus into a religion *about* Jesus. Instead of following his example and attaining "cosmic consciousness," followers have eclipsed the original good news of Jesus. Watts argues, "Jesus was not the man he was as a result of making Jesus Christ his personal savior." The religion *of* Jesus is to realize that each of us is a Son of God, just as Christ did. *Son of* here means "of the nature of" so that each individual ought to come to realize that he is One with God.[30]

In Watts' view, orthodox Christian theologians have (erroneously) asserted that *who* Christ was and is remains more important than what he said. Jesus has become a "fetish" which has spiritually paralyzed orthodox Christianity. For Watts, to have true faith in Jesus is to have him in us and to be in him in the same sense the bird is in the air and the air in the bird. But orthodox Christianity has misunderstood all that. Concludes Watts, "Poor Jesus! If he had known how great an authority was to be projected upon him, he would never have said a word."[31]

The doctrine of original sin has also been misunderstood. If it means anything, asserts Watts, it means that infants are brainwashed into believing that survival is a frantic necessity. Original sin is the malady taught us by adult reactions and attitudes which causes us to think that certain experiences of tension are actually "painful" or "bad" simply because they form a prelude to death, an event which should be greatly feared.[32]

The ultimate solution to original sin is likewise suspect. If this life is real, God becomes the Final End for which everything else exists. But to think of eternal life as a future reward is unrealistic; the future remains eternally unattainable. Like the proverbial dangled carrot, it is always ahead of the donkey. For Watts, fulfillment of our purpose in life does not lie in the future but in the present, in seeing that truly no individual exists.[33]

Among the most obnoxious elements of Christianity, according to Watts, are the interests in petitionary prayers and "spiritual imperialism." Though we might "focus the psychic energy of the congregation upon given individuals," drawing the attention of an omniscient God to the cancerous body of Aunt Susan will be useless: if God really exists he would already know about the cancer and thus would be able to do far more to cure the problem than any of the petitioners. But the fact is, argues Watts, Aunt Susan is really God in disguise, "playing hide-and-seek with himself at an extreme end of the spectrum of 'hide,' at which extreme point Aunt Susan may well do a flip and discover who and what she really is."[34]

Watts finds the church's craze for making converts even more offensive. The claim to be the best religion is "proud and arbitrary," and Christianity should stop sending missionaries to convert the "heathen," especially when the missionaries know next to nothing of the indigenous faiths and religions.[35]

One positive facet of Christianity lies in its moral and ethical imperatives. "Thou shalt love the Lord thy God!" is an impossible commandment which accentuates the illusion of separate egos and conscious will power to an absurd extreme. Thus Christianity's many ethical imperatives put the Christian into an existential double-bind and act as the proscenium arch, the crack in the wall that helps us see through the illusion of separated egos. At the extreme point of absurdity the illusion can explode into a discovery of humanity's eternal identity with the Lord.[36] In a word, Watts complains that modern Christianity is simply unrealistic, always misunderstanding the true meaning of the religion of Jesus Christ: "The Christ who walks with me and talks with me is not the Christ within; he is the crutch, not the backbone."[37]

The True Place of Religion. Twentieth-century Christianity misunderstands its function as a religion, claims Watts. Religion should never be a set of predictions about the future. Doctrines in general exist not in the realm of the future and the everlasting but in the arena of the present and the eternal. Dogma should be a series of graphic symbols expressing present experience. When theologians assert the existence of God, they are really proposing a hypothesis to explain human existence. Thereby, argues Watts, they enter the field of science, use the techniques of science and yield results which are open to the criticism and scrutiny of "fellow naturalists." A more useful distinction between religion and science would be to define *nature* as the world which thought has analyzed, measured and sorted into groups. The supernatural realm of religion would then consist of the absolute reality behind the names and categories. There is no way to define or describe *what* it is, although we can be aware of it at every moment. True religion deals with a reality which can only be felt and sensed; trying to define that reality is like "trying to make a knife cut itself."[38]

This distinction between the study of nature and the apprehension of the supernatural, parallels a contrast between belief and faith. Belief, asserts Watts implies some tangible content that must be positively asserted as the idea that is to be believed, but faith cannot deal in the realm of positive verbalization.[39] A believer will accept the truth of a certain statement on the condition that it corresponds to his preconceived notions. But faith must unreservedly open the mind to the truth, whatever it turns out to be. No preconceptions inhibit faith, for faith plunges into the unknown. In a word, "belief clings, but faith lets go."[40]

Such a view of the function of true religion puts positive statements of dogmatic belief on a very low plane. As the masters of Zen Buddhism often implied, the teaching of any spiritual mentor serves only to point the way toward the goal of religion. Categorical description, like a raft, serves well to get one to the far side of a river, but the raft must be left behind once the far bank is reached if the journey is to be continued. Religion requires that one give up the security of dogmatic statements, for, according to Watts, relinquishing categorical assertions means gaining an apprehension of truth. As Christ said, "He that loses his life will find it!"[41]

Christianity depends too heavily upon its dogmatic statements. Although such dependence provides security, it necessarily stunts spiritual growth. Dogmatic forms are not necessarily contrary to religion, but they must not usurp the place of the true meaning of mystical intuition. They must be used in their impermanent, transient form to reach the far bank of the river, the realm where categorical assertions give way to the feeling, sensing apprehension of the Oneness that has always existed.[42]

Summary

Several summary comments will help tie together Watts' view of pantheism and Christianity. First, there can be no doubt that many Christian mystics through the centuries have come close to asserting a pantheistic system. Huxley claims Meister Eckhart as an adherent of the *Philosophia Perennis*, and D. T. Suzuki takes pains to point out the closeness of Eckhart's thought to that of Mahayana Buddhism, particularly Zen.[43] Clearly, the *Philosophia Perennis* remains a position which exhibits surface appeal and which gives some evidence to support its contention that mystics everywhere have argued for a unified view of reality: it is not necessarily self-evident that Christianity and pantheism are incompatible.

Second, however, Watts' later writings demonstrate that he understands Christianity's claims to uniqueness. He argues that the Christian concept of creatures which come out of nowhere into existence is, upon reflection, "a freak of imagination without any parallel in nature." Even when we say people are "poles apart," argues Watts, we are still implying that there is some fundamental element of relationship.[44] Christians "anthropomorphize" God when they think of themselves in terms of individual egos in "bags of skin." When they construct a God in their own human image, they are only exhibiting their own poor self-image. We need to visualize persons as activity in a unified field so that God can be conceived of in that same image. Delving deeper into oneself means going farther out into the universe, until one reaches a point where our three-dimensional, sensible outlook is no longer valid.[45]

Christianity has created a problem by perpetuating the monarchial and paternal concept of Yahweh. God in this image represents the creation of peoples who were accustomed to Oriental potentates with their nose-scraping subjects. Watts predicted that within a few decades this imagery would seem as "superstitious as flat-earthism." This imagery, which so grossly misrepresents the way things really are, must be avoided, so that our true existence as a unified whole can be finally understood. When we transcend the ego-illusion, we will finally come to realize that at root each of us is one with all the other branches.[46]

Third, the *Philosophia Perennis* and the Chinese box notwithstanding, Christianity is (rightly or wrongly) incurably theistic. To hold that pantheism is compatible with theism is impossible; any group that claims to possess the truth implicitly denies any claim which conflicts with its own.[47] It is clearly and plainly contradictory to hold that all men and women are God playing hide-and-seek and at the same time to assert that the Creator/creature distinction is real and not merely formal. One cannot hold both positions even if it is true that faith has no positive, tangible content. Therefore a choice must be made: it may be possible to reject both the theistic and the pantheistic models in favor of a third, but it is clearly impossible to hold these together, even in some sort of synthesis.

After many attempts at just such a synthesis, Watts finally came to believe that Christianity put him in a double-bind by forcing him to love when he simply could not love. He decided then that he would have to stop trying to be a Christian. At Millbrook he wrote, "At a yet deeper level, the more I see the futility of myself clinging to myself, I have no choice but to stop clinging."[48] Thus Watts questioned the plausibility of a universe conceived as an eternal monarchy, complete with its everlasting dungeon or torture chamber.[49] As Watts clearly saw, we must make a choice.

4

KNOWLEDGE
OF
REALITY

Ultimate reality, for Watts, lies beyond conceptual distinctions and therefore yields to insight only in the intuition of mystical experience. This intuition takes place in a "sudden awakening" or, to use D. T. Suzuki's term, a *satori*.[1] *Satori*, the Japanese word for "knowledge," became for Watts the key method by which the nature of true reality can be apprehended. Before *satori* can take place, however, an essential negative aspect of knowing must first be accomplished through the use of the *koan*, the Zen paradox.

Koan: The Technique of Zen

Mystics have often disparaged the value of the intellect. Many tend to radically differentiate the "pseudoknowledge" acquired by our normal processes of intellection and sensation from the true type of knowledge that is the result of mystical intuition. As Christmas Humphreys has asserted, Zen belongs entirely in the realm of intuition, transcending the categorical statements that are the basis of all description and argument. Only lesser writers and thinkers (including some who are considered intellectual giants in the academic world) attempt to conceptualize ultimate reality. But such an enterprise is doomed to failure. Like Zen itself, reality can no more be explained than a joke. Either you see it or you do not. No middle ground exists.[2]

This approach to statements about reality reduces all formalizations, theories and dogmatic creeds and systems to lifeless formality. These formal systems are merely ideas *about* the truth; they eternally doom attempts at direct contact with reality itself by standing between the knower and the known, preventing their direct contact.[3]

This deprecation of intellectual thought, however, should not be taken to mean that such reasoning is of no value whatsoever. On the one hand, a Zen master must never allow the disciple to forget that one must cross the river which separates real knowledge from that which can be expressed. On the other hand, it is also true that the Western mind needs discursive description to lead him by the hand to the edge of that river.[4] When we use a raft (dogmatic statements) to cross the river to the far bank of reality (the area of true meaning beyond thought and speech), we must be careful to remember that the raft is but an inadequate means to a far greater goal. We must abandon the raft and move on. Therefore, just as "the law was our schoolmaster to bring us to Christ," so categorical explanation brings us to Zen.[5]

The Necessity of Experience. Genuine apprehension of reality has to do with personal, firsthand experience. Someone else's experience is at best secondhand, and thus, while it may be a signpost which can point the way, it should never be mistaken for the path itself, much less the goal. True and living reality can be known only by immediate personal experience.[6]

It is for this reason that the wisdom of the East always finds its basis in psychological experiment. Revelation invariably grounds the theologies of the West, but in the East the profound sense of unity between God and humanity arises from the experiments into the consciousness of the mind. According to Watts, long before the Western psychologists had invented the concept of the subconscious, philosophers of India and China had devised experiments to expand and deepen those areas of everyday experience which are "screened out" by conscious attention. While some Western mystics have attempted a study of the subconscious, according to Watts, the sophistication of these attempts cannot hope to match that of the detailed studies of the Eastern thinkers.[7]

The experimental approach supersedes the approach of revelation which provides the content in traditional Christianity. Revelation resides in the area of the conscious intellect, providing the mind with dogmas to be believed and understood. This approach is unrealistic; it assumes that during those ages when revelations were given, men and women somehow had a keener awareness of God than at other times and other places. Concludes Watts, the best way to choose a world view in the twentieth-century intellectual climate should be that of psychological experiment, not of arbitrary, antiquated, fixated revelation.[8]

Despite the rudimentary usefulness accorded to discursive reasoning, the basic conclusion of this discussion is that words (as well as theories and conceptual ideas) are less than real. Concepts will never serve as adequate substitutes for immediate knowledge, argues Humphreys, and we should therefore abandon even the attempt to feed our desire for immediate knowledge with the "truth of Zen." Zen never has concepts which make up statements of truth: "Words have their uses, but the noblest words are but noises in the air. They die, and in the end is silence, silence and a finger pointing the Way."[9]

What is obviously needed, then, is an experience of the sort that will distinguish itself from the bifurcated, conceptual experience that we have become accustomed to. For Watts, immediate learning of the nature of reality "involves a far more acute awareness of the plain evidence of the senses than is usual." This "acute awareness" never retreats into the shelter of private experience and subjectivity but finds that its total interest is the transcending of subjectivity. It awakens persons to the realm of the concrete and actual, as opposed to what is merely abstract and conceptual. Those who undertake this approach to reality "unanimously report a vision of the world startlingly different from that of the average socially conditioned man." Concludes Watts, the frustrations of our spatio-temporal existence turn out to be illusion.[10]

The Challenges of Paradox. The tangle of consciousness as we know it, with its fruitless goals (e.g., pie-in-the-sky eternal life) and frustrating experiences (e.g., sickness and fear of death), must be transcended. The contradictions of conceptual description must be wiped out to make room for the immediate experience that will open up the true nature of reality. To find release from this convention, Zen vigorously asserts the need to break down the merely intellectual images of true reality. The *koan*, the Zen paradox, is the means by which to accomplish the destruction of conventional modes of experience.

A *koan* (such as the classic one: What is the sound of one hand clapping?) never amounts to a mere pun, which is a phrase resolvable by the simple exposure of the double meaning of a certain word. Instead of arising from the desire to amuse or mystify, the *koan* arises out of the inability of language to include opposite ideas in a single statement. Amputation of a leg causes pain and loss, but it also saves a life. It is nearly impossible to express (or even to conceive) a good/bad action in a single idea. The conceptual habits of the mind immediately interpret a single event in two, distinct segments. The Bible contains many paradoxes which are halting attempts to express the double-edged meaning of what is actually the case. Christ asserted, "He who finds his life will lose it, and he who loses his life for my sake will find it!"

Just so, a *koan* expresses more than would a pun; it is an expression of a single idea which our conceptual framework unwittingly divides.[11]

Watts himself, after noting that mysticism must contain antinomies and paradoxes to be complete, admitted that at the base of his metaphysical world view there lies genuine paradox:

If union is to be perfect, God must be in the most intimate and inseparable union not only with the soul but also with its entire experience of life and the world. But if that with which the soul is united is to be God, he must at the same time be infinitely above, beyond, and other than the soul and the world. Furthermore, if God is the source and height of liveliness and creative power, he cannot be anything less than a person, since a law or principle is simply an automatic, mechanical, and dead mode of behaviour. On the other hand, if God is the ultimate Reality, the one source of all things, he must be free from the limitation of personality as we know it, and must not be subject to the mutability and the limitations of the forms in which his creative activity is expressed.[12]

Although Watts admits that paradoxes of this magnitude lie at the heart of the pantheistic world view, he does not think this presents any conceptual difficulties. According to Watts, the paradox itself serves to show, not the inadequacy of a certain viewpoint, but that the whole enterprise of discursive reasoning (which is the source of the antinomy) cannot function to describe reality. The Zen masters use such paradoxes to produce a *koan* which puts disciples into a double-bind which indicates to our intuition the illusory nature of conceptualizations. In this way one can be freed from the chains of brain thinking.[13]

The *koan* is the device which Zen masters have used for centuries to mire their students in a logical cul-de-sac. It represents a formal problem based on the actions or words of the master. It cannot be answered intellectually; any attempt at a logical response thrusts the student toward a dead end which brings about a state of acute despair and frustration. The *koan* therefore is never a trance-inducing activity but is merely a means of breaking through the barrier of conceptual thought.[14]

The method of the *koan* is not to make the nature of true reality understandable; it is quite the opposite. *The method of Zen is to baffle, excite, puzzle and exhaust the intellect until it is realized that intellection is only thinking about; it will provoke, irritate and again exhaust the emotions until it is realized that emotion is only feeling about, and then it contrives, when the disciple has been brought to an intellectual and emotional impasse, to bridge the gap between second-hand, conceptual contact with reality, and first-hand experience.*[15]

Watts argues that Christianity has a *koan* built right into its system. The intensification of the sense of individual existence brought on by morbid guilt (in Protestantism) or by God's regal glory (in Catholicism) can so increase in weight that it is like building pressure behind a dam. When the water rises high enough, the dam bursts and there is a sudden awareness that the dam should never have been erected in the first place. The *koan* challenges the Zen disciple to demonstrate the power and independence of his presumed ego. But when this enterprise leads to dilemmas on every hand, the disciple learns suddenly to laugh at the cosmic joke, just as the master has been doing all along.[16]

The *koan* thus serves an important negative function on the road to true knowledge. It clears the deck of the mind, eliminating the entanglements and paradoxes that arise because of categorical thought, making room for a psychic life that can work at a deeper and more powerful level. Thus whenever the Zen master answers a disciple's query by beating the disciple with a stick, by asking another question, by laughing uproariously or by totally ignoring the question, the implicitly conveyed meaning is, "Don't think; don't use your discursive intellect; don't reason; true knowledge develops in a different realm of your psyche from all this."[17] As a means of communicating something to the disciple, the *koan* has been the tool by which Zen is propagated. Despite its lack of explicit content, Zen has somehow been passed on from master to disciple for centuries. That Zen tacitly communicates content by means of the *koan* is a point we shall develop later.

Satori: The Heart of Zen
Once the spadework has been finished there is room for positive attainment in immediate knowledge. Because the *koan* has eliminated the illusory sort of knowledge based on the conceptual, dualistic realm of the mind, there arises the opportunity for a supra-conceptual, intuitional knowledge. This knowledge is attained in the experience called *satori*.

The Purpose of Satori. Clearly from the above discussion, Watts holds that one major problem with our society is its dependence on the pigeonholes of intellectual frameworks. Brain thinking has increased, dominating our lives out of all proportion to its real importance while instinctual wisdom has atrophied.

Liberation from the duality inspired by conceptual thinking (which is the aim of all Buddhism, according to Watts) brings with it a totally new, synoptic way of viewing reality. For this reason proponents of Zen consider themselves neither "atheists" nor "pantheists" for the application of these terms implies the dualistic framework of the applier: this schema itself must be rejected.

With the elimination of dualistic thought, there remains no ego which can be desired for its own sake. The individual ego is like a shell which explodes at the moment of *satori*. The individual does not become suddenly absorbed into the One Ego. Rather, one's individuality, as something kept separate from other individual existences, becomes somehow loosened, and without its tightening grip, existence "melts away into something indescribable."[18] In other words, the change which takes place in *satori* is epistemological not ontological, one of knowing not being. Usually we do not realize that our situation as solitary egos in opposition to an alien environment arises from a contradiction inherent in the conventional rules of the cosmic game. Most of us believe that, as some existentialists would say, we are "beings unto death." But according to Watts, this pseudoproblem resulted from a false step in our biological adaptation which may have seemed quite promising at first. Thus liberation awaits those who feel they can no longer tolerate their anxiety and guilt. These sensations may themselves be a *koan* which could help one to realize "that he, the agent, cannot act, does not act, and never did act. There is just action—Tao."[19]

Such a sudden realization of the true nature of reality corresponds to proscenium arches which give a cue to the unified nature of reality. These are sudden slips into another dimension or "wavelength" which impress those who experience them as being more real than conceptually mediated experience. Thus the purpose of *satori* is to see through the Christian roulette game where the stakes are everlasting life and death. With the immediate experience of *satori* one can notice the occasional crack in the wall or have the chance to see "behind the scenes" and find out that the drama, by its very nature, should not be taken with ultimate seriousness.[20]

Describing the Satori. Satori has been defined simply as an "intuitive looking into the nature of things in contradistinction to the analytical or logical understanding of it." Practically speaking, *satori* unfolds an entirely new world which usually goes unperceived because of the confusion in our dualistically trained minds. Though this may seem impossible, *satori* unites all opposites and distinctions into an organic whole. The standpoint of logic cannot be accepted as finally authoritative. One who has experienced *satori* views his surroundings from an unexpected angle of perception. After *satori* the old world is never quite the same.[21]

While *satori* is theoretically indescribable, it is certainly not indefinite in the manner of its effects upon the individual who experiences it. Essentially *satori* is a sudden experience which can be described as a "turning over" of the mind. When the weight of conceptual arguments is placed in the pan on one side of a pair of scales, the balance shifts. But that shifting can always be counterbalanced by the weight of another conceptual argument in the other pan. But if sufficient weight is put in one side, the scales will suddenly flip completely over, and the entire standard of measurement will become inoperable and no longer valid.[22]

Remembering that *satori* cannot truly be described, Watts does his best to express its significance. *Satori* cannot be defined because it represents a sudden, intuitive understanding of the "truth" of Zen that nothing can truly be asserted about what is.[23] It is for this reason that Zen masters have abandoned the activity of making assertions about reality; they do not even make the positive assertion, "No positive assertions can be made about reality!" They seem to realize that such statement would itself be a positive assertion. Instead they leave the seeker of wisdom to stumble over a *koan* until the apprehension of true reality breaks into his consciousness and the scales of categorical thought do a complete flip.

Watts describes *satori*, like conversion in Christianity, as an abrupt affair that breaks very suddenly over one's consciousness after a long struggle with a *koan*. One grapples with a *koan* from a master until one reaches the impasse where the end of human mental limits lies. There, like a person hanging over a precipice, one is at a total loss as to what to do next. Suddenly one finds mind, body and the *koan* itself wiped out of existence. This is what the masters call "letting go your hold"; as we have mentioned, "belief clings, but faith lets go." A Zen master once concluded, "Nothing is left to you at this moment but to burst out into a loud laugh."[24]

Probably the most important aspect of the *satori* experience is its noncognitive nature. The apprehension of reality gained in *satori* is decidedly different from the knowledge available through discursive reasoning. Rather, the true knowledge of *satori* is intuitive; it dwells on the meaning behind thoughts and words. Notes Watts, meaning is itself meaningless because it does not *have* meaning (as words do) but *is* meaning. A tree, by itself, is meaningless because it is the meaning of the word "tree." Just so, the true attainment of *satori* is beyond meaning and concepts in the realm of undifferentiated wisdom.[25]

How to Attain Satori. The attempt to reach a *satori* results in paradox for the disciple who wants to work positively toward that goal. Zen interprets positive striving for *satori* to be an admission that one is separated from the surrounding environment. One who strives for Buddhahood presupposes duality between himself and Buddhahood and is thereby thrust into the existential double-bind. Striving for the solution to the problem of duality shows only that duality is still guiding the striver's mind. Concludes Watts, this is a form of lunacy, in that the lunatic is a person who is isolated from the world.[26]

The solution to this double-bind obviously cannot be another positive action. For example, one must not *try* to stop trying to attain *satori*. Such striving would heighten the sense of isolation, compounding the problem. There must rather be a negative action in order to attain *satori*. The process of "letting go" must be expressed negatively as *not* trying to grasp something to believe: "Furthermore, such 'letting-go' faith must come about not as a positive work to be done, but through the realization that there is really nothing else to do, since it is actually impossible to grasp the inmost being."[27]

Watts argues that this negative action is inherent in Christianity. In his early writings, he held that Christianity, like swimming, requires a certain amount of relaxation ("letting go") of the soul to God. Without this giving of oneself to God in the negative sense, God's offer of union through the Incarnation ("at-one-ment") would never be fully realized.[28]

The best way to get out of the vicious circle of ego-illusion is not by trying harder and harder to get out of the circle. This is exactly what makes the circle turn. If we feel separated from the life process around us, then we feel driven to survive and the continuation of life becomes our highest duty. But it also becomes a drag which, when accomplished, never quite lives up to its original billing. Thus we feel trapped, paralyzed, unable to escape from a game which, when taken too seriously, results in double-binds at every hand. This sense of paralysis, like a *koan*, becomes the dawning realization that this approach to life is nonsense and that the idea of independent egos is a fiction. "I" simply do not exist, and when we realize that we are not detached observers, we can "let go" and let *satori* happen.

No-Mind: The Goal of Zen

Buddhism finds the extinction of desire to be the final way to escape the problems of this life. This goal has been called *Nirvana*, the state of knowing that reality is beyond the finitude and bondage of this world.[29]

Zen No-Mind. The idea of nothingness or emptiness is well known as the goal of Buddhism. But for a major proponent of Rinzai Zen, D. T. Suzuki, this notion must be qualified so as not to imply a dualistic view of the universe. For example, the emptiness (*sunyata*, the same "no-thing-ness" out of which, according to Watts, God created) of the mind can easily be misunderstood as mere absence. The lack of hair on the turtle's back does *not* illustrate the emptiness of no-mind. Nor does no-mind mean extinction in the sense of a fire which was once burning but has now gone out. The idea of vacancy falls short of expressing no-mind. The uncluttered section of a generally cluttered room cannot illustrate true *sunyata*. Absence, extinction and unoccupancy fall short, for they are on the plane of relativity; that is, they are emptiness as opposed to fullness.

Zen no-mind is Absolute Emptiness transcending all

forms of mutual relationship, subject/object, birth/death, God/world and affirmation/negation. This Absolute Emptiness entails no time, no space, no becoming, no-thing-ness. Zen *sunyata* is a "zero full of infinite possibilities, it is a void of inexhaustible contents."[30]

For this same reason, Zen is not considered to be a pantheism, according to Suzuki. He admits that some biased critics seem simple-minded enough to lump all nontranscendent or nonmonotheistic religions into one undifferentiated category. But Suzuki argues that Zen is neither a pantheism nor an atheism, because both of these labels are used only by those who accept the dualistic view of things, and thus they do damage to true Zen.[31]

Whatever Suzuki and others say about Zen, one thing seems clear: Zen is not a theism which contains a Being worthy of worship. While it may not ultimately deny God's existence, it swallows him (it) up in *sunyata*, removing him entirely from the realm of inquiry.[32] The basic category of no-mind does not exist in contrast to other categories, for there is no mutual exclusion of any kind. The Absolute Emptiness transcends all forms of mutual exclusion or relationship, including the polar relationships which form Watts' basic polar/field view of reality.

Watts' Relationship to Zen

How Watts actually relates to the notions of Zen Buddhism seems difficult to pinpoint because the writings from different periods in his life reflect differing emphases. One of the most significant differences between Hindu and Buddhist thought is an issue on which Watts seemed to shift during his middle years. The Hindu concept of *atman*, the individual self, which is connected to *Brahman*, the cosmic Self, is something which exists substantially. A "substance," in Western thought, is an unchanging reality which underlies the "accidents," the changing outward qualities or characteristics. The distinction between substance and accidents can be found in the Catholic doctrine of transubstantiation where the substances of the bread and wine (the underlying realities) are actually changed into the substances of the body and blood, despite the fact that the accidents (the outward qualities) remain those of bread and wine. For the Hindus, the individual soul, *atman* (which is really one with *Brahman*, the universe) is an unchanging substance which lies behind the realm of experiences.[33]

The concept of the individual self held by most Buddhists differs from this substantial view. Many Buddhists hold to the notion of *anatman*, "no-mind" or "no-soul." This view asserts that there exists no unchanging subject behind or beneath the processes of experience. When one walks, there exists a holistic process which should not be divided into walker (static subject) and walking (active process). One cannot assign genuine ontological status to the walker for the walker does not exist independently of the process of walking. There is only the whole, undifferentiated movement of walking. The walker is only an abstraction from the total process.

Watts, in his earlier writings, seems to assign real status to the various poles of existence. There seems to be real ontological connections between two real poles. His free use of the Hindu terms *Brahman* and *atman*, without guarding against their substantialistic connotations, implies his belief in real, underlying realities. This substantial view fits well with the *Philosophia Perennis*, and Watts' open-hearted espousal of the *Philosophia Perennis* may be seen as a sign that he felt that a real underlying reality did actually exist as the subject of experiences.

Logically, Watts' de-emphasis of the *Philosophia Perennis* and consequent rejection of Christianity (Watts held on to Christianity only when he felt it was a different *form* which described the same *meaning* as other religions), follows from his acceptance of the Buddhist notion of *anatman*, "no-mind." That he did come to hold this nonsubstantial idea is confirmed by statements which he made just two weeks before his death. In an interview, Watts stated, "Life is insubstantial. . . . If I can buy the idea of myself as a figment of my imagination, I can relax. Living is like a dream. . . . [There is] no ego [identity] separate from the rest of reality."[34]

This shift in metaphysical viewpoint did not seem to affect Watts' view of the mystical epistemology or way of knowing. Throughout his writings, both before and after his change of heart at Millbrook, Watts borrowed the basic terminology of Zen mysticism. He used Zen epistemology, probably due to the influence of D. T. Suzuki, to support first his more Hindu, substantialist view of reality, and later his more Buddhist, nonsubstantialist view of egos and reality. But both these metaphysical views, despite their difference on the question of substance, can be generally classed as pantheistic. On the Hindu model, *Brahman* is the cosmic Self that is connected to all the individual selves; on the Buddhist model, all of reality is one complex, interrelated process of movement and experience, although it lacks independent "experiencers" or subjects who remain constant through the changing process. In general, Watts' attitude toward specific Eastern religious traditions and his emphasis on the personal adaptation or interpretation of any particular system of belief can best be seen in this statement: "I do not even style myself a Zen Buddhist, for the aspect of Zen in which I am personally interested is nothing that can be organized, taught, transmitted, certified, or wrapped up in any kind of system. It can't even be followed, for everyone has to find it for himself."[35]

Summary

To summarize Watts' basic epistemology we will make several concluding remarks. First, at the most basic level, knowledge for Watts is based on mystical experiment. Naturally he must make a distinction between differing types of experience because our sense of individual identity is also based on experience. Thus, while not all experience leads to knowledge, all knowledge is based on experience. As Watts wrote, a metaphysic of the kind he holds to *involves a far more acute awareness of the plain evidence of the senses than is usual, and . . . so far from retreating into a subjective and private world of its own, its entire concern is to transcend subjectivity, so that man may "wake up" to the world which is concrete and actual, as distinct from that which is purely abstract and conceptual.*[36]

Second, a corollary follows naturally from this first remark. If true reality cannot be bound by the laws of logic (as our minds are bound) then the apprehensions of our minds, knowledge which conforms to logic, cannot be knowledge of true reality. That is, if logic applies to our way of thinking, but not to reality, then the relationship between our way of thinking and reality itself becomes problematic. Watts obviously holds this to be the case. What we need is not more conceptual assertions about reality but "the Absolute behind the relative, the Meaning behind thoughts and words." Since the thoughts and the words we normally use are limited by logic, they never reach reality. What we need is Meaning itself, which, unlike words, does not *have* meaning but *is* meaning.[37]

Third, true knowledge, as for most mystics, is ineffable. Just as we cannot explain the beauty of a sunset to someone who has been blind from birth, so it is impossible to find the words which will adequately express the mystical experience to one who has not experienced it firsthand. In the words of the Zen masters, the "chariot of speech" often finds no track to follow. Therefore, in answer to all religious questions one ought only to offer silence: "Silence—and a finger pointing the Way."[38]

Fourth, knowledge about the ultimate reality necessarily exhibits paradoxical elements. D. T. Suzuki provides an extreme case when he gives the example of the two masters, Daizui and Shu, who were asked exactly the same question.

One answered the question "yes," while the other answered "no." Suzuki comments that from a logical standpoint, these two answers seem irreconcilable. But from the standpoint of the highest reality, it is still possible to claim that Zen teachings are consistent, for Zen is primarily interested in its experience and only secondarily in its modes of expression. Whenever experience is expressed, paradoxes, contradictions and ambiguities are bound to arise.[39]

5

AN
EVALUATION
OF WATTS

Watts correctly saw in his later writings that Christianity is incorrigibly theistic and that therefore one could not be a Christian (at least in the sense in which Christianity has traditionally been understood) and still be a pantheist. Watts held (correctly, from a logical standpoint) that the two metaphysical world views excluded one another and that they cannot be simultaneously held by a single, consistent individual.

This raises an important point which will later become significant. If Watts really implicitly rejected logic in his argumentation as he did in his explicit statements on the value of logical distinctions, he would have no reason to make this concession. Watts here seems to be admitting that the *Philosophia Perennis* has exceptions. Not all religions fit into the *Philosophia Perennis,* and the only reason this could be so is that contrary statements about reality cannot both be true in the same sense and at the same time. If there are two mutually exclusive ways of viewing reality (as Watts' rejection of Christianity seems to imply), then we are put in the position of having to choose between world views. This in turn implies that there be standards or criteria by which to make the choice.

The Problem of Criteria

As every baseball fan knows, deciding the rules of the game before the first pitch is tossed can turn out to be very important when the score is tied in the ninth inning. In the same way, criticisms of a certain world view must be careful to follow certain rules if they are to successfully evaluate a view other than that held by the critic. Some have warned, for example, that any criticism of Zen which presupposes a division between matter and spirit is bound to go astray because of that very presupposition.[1] In more general terms, when two competing world views come into conflict, it is hard to state the issues and criticisms without begging the question in favor of one side or the other. It becomes very difficult to judge between world views on grounds which are entirely neutral.[2]

Watts himself notes this problem and states it in its strongest form when he asserts that there is "no satisfactory way of arguing the merits of any one of the great world religions against the others." Such debates, writes Watts, are often hopelessly biased because the "judge and the advocate are the same person, for a man judges his own religion the best simply because the standard he uses is that of his own religious upbringing." Thus the apologetic approaches of many religions toward each other seem to reduce to tedious circularity.[3]

Watts therefore challenges his readers to find criteria for the religious choice independent of the viewpoint they happen to hold. The Christian who maintains that his own position is superior to some other religion "must not forget that he bases his judgment upon standards which he has acquired from Christianity—so that his conclusion is foregone or, more plainly, prejudiced." There is no excuse for "provincialism," concludes Watts; we should now require, as the "bare minimum of theological competency, a thorough understanding of religious traditions outside Christianity."[4]

Watts' Criterion: Plausibility. Watts recognized this problem and proposed a criterion, but he did not claim to be able to reach the ultimate Truth by applying this criterion. In fact, he asserted that in the twentieth century it seems "simply inept and boorish to claim that a certain philosophical or theological position is 'the Truth' and still more so to attempt to prove it." If there is anything we do know, says Watts, we know one thing for sure, and that is that we do not know very much. Mystical experiences do give a sense of psychological certitude in support of ontological identity, but we must still exercise caution when expressing such certainty in propositional form. So Watts concludes, "It is one thing to have an authentic vision of the stars, but quite another to deliver an accurate description of their relative positions."[5]

Watts does, however, tentatively offer one criterion which can be used to eliminate certain world views: "My own feeling is that the most that should be claimed for any metaphysic, theology or cosmology which is trying to say something about the way things are, about how the universe works, is plausibility."[6] If everlasting damnation were really a possibility, then certitude would be a valuable goal to pursue. But such divine retribution is far-fetched and thus certainty is unnecessary. What we need is the adaptability and courage of a gambler, not the fixed convictions and creeds of the legalistic religious believer; we do not need firm ground to stand on, but we do need skill in swimming.[7]

What does it mean for a world view to be "plausible"? Is this a psychological term or a logical one? Watts seems to suggest by his use of this criterion that plausibility is indeed a logical notion. To be plausible, a world view must consistently explain the sum total of human experience of reality within its own guidelines. These guidelines do not necessarily have to be logical ones, for some world views consistently resist logic. But for a particular world view which ultimately rejects logic, no (apparently) opposing world views or contrary statements can be eliminated simply because they contradict that world view. If someone does reject another world view or metaphysical statement because it contradicts his own, he has implicitly incorporated within his guidelines the necessities of logic.

Watts does precisely this: by rejecting certain world views which are logically contrary to his own, he suggests the validity of logic. Implausibility for him becomes something more than a psychological criterion: the world view presupposed by Christianity fails because its logical implications for daily life are distasteful. For example, Watts claims that the concept of God as a personal being somehow outside this world produces problems; it is too much of a good thing. When schoolchildren are working at their desks and even a kindly teacher looks over their shoulders, they usually feel rather uneasy. It must be even more disconcerting to realize that every single deed, thought and feeling is being watched by the Teacher of teachers, and that there is no hiding place from God's eye anywhere in the universe.[8] In this case, the problem with Christian theism lies in the realm of its implication for daily life. Watts' complaint with the Christian God resides in the sphere of logical meaning. In order for a world view to be plausible (as Watts uses the criterion), it has to be at least liveable and meaningful.

We will use, therefore, as part of our basic standard of judgment, the criterion of plausibility. It may at this point be objected that plausibility is too weak a criterion to be used in the choice between theism and pantheism. In response it will be granted that plausibility is a weak criterion in a positive sense. If a world view is plausible this fact by itself may not be enough to establish it as ultimately true. On the other hand, if a world view can be rendered implausible the criticism is extremely powerful. Like the test of internal consistency, plausibility may not be exclusive enough to be the only test between all world views, but any world view which fails the test of plausibility has been decisively eliminated.

Criticisms of the Polar/Field Metaphysic

In presenting Watts' world view, we discussed three general areas of his system. First, we spoke of the metaphysical system of pantheism itself. Second, we mentioned Watts' view (and its evolution) concerning the relationship between pantheism and Christianity. Third, we discussed Watts' epistemology, which he described in language borrowed from the Zen Buddhists. This evaluation of Watts will follow these three general areas.

Circular or Biased Criticisms. Many of the criticisms which have been leveled at the pantheistic world view fail, for they either presuppose another world view or they bring up issues which the pantheistic system either admits or can remedy, at least in principle. We will mention several of these criticisms.

First, pantheism has been criticized because it does not agree with the conclusion of the theistic arguments. According to this criticism, to hold pantheism requires certain sacrifices, one of which is that "all the arguments . . . to show the existence of God . . . must be discarded."[9] But this criticism ignores several important points. To begin with, a mystical pantheist like Watts can deny that intellection ever gives valid knowledge about anything real without making his system internally incoherent. Watts can hold that such argumentation necessarily presupposes a duality of knower and known which reduces it to invalidity. Moreover, many of those in the history of philosophy who have used "theistic" arguments have reached something besides a strictly transcendent God. Independent arguments must show that the conclusion of these arguments cannot support pantheism. Finally, the persuasiveness, if not the validity of these arguments, has been gravely undermined in today's philosophical climate. Their conclusion is by no means foregone.

Second, pantheism has been criticized for its idealistic nature. According to Flint, this is a sacrifice that must be made to believe pantheism. Pantheism identifies thought and existence and thus calls on us to reject material objects which cannot be conceived of except as distinct from thought.[10] But this is weak for several reasons. Pantheists often admit that their system is idealistic. Zen Buddhists say no sound is made by a tree falling in the forest unless a mind hears it. While this may seem strange to Westerners, it by no means decisively eliminates pantheism. Moreover, historically pantheism has been held by some fervent non-idealists. Probably the most notable example was the seventeenth-century Jewish rationalist, Benedict Spinoza.

Third, some have mentioned as a criticism that pantheism is equivalent to atheism. For all practical purposes, pantheism is an atheistic system of belief, for while it may not absolutely deny God's existence, it at least removes him (it) from our field of inquiry. If "God" is not a transcendent, personal Creator, but everything that is, then he (it) is not "God" at all.[11] This criticism also has several problems. Pantheists admit, without creating incoherency in their system, that a personal God modeled after the ancient Eastern monarchs does not exist. Watts thinks this model is ridiculous. Furthermore, this criticism is basically a difference of opinion as to the definition of *God*. The critics may be correct in that using the word *God* to denote the whole universe goes against customary linguistic usage. But this by itself does not damage the pantheistic world view in principle.

Fourth, some have argued that pantheism is inadequate because its God is not personal. The ultimate in many pantheistic systems is an impersonal force, being or mind which spontaneously creates emanationally, out of its own being. But several factors keep this criticism from being decisive. To begin with, it is not crucial to the pantheistic system that the ultimate be impersonal. In fact, many pantheists, Watts included, often speak of reality in personal terms. (Watts does so despite his rejection of monarchial imagery, a fact which makes one wonder if he has a legitimate basis for speaking of God in personal terms.) Then, too, even if the pantheistic God is impersonal, that criticism is of little consequence unless the critic can demonstrate that there is something conceptually inadequate about the idea of an impersonal ultimate. The criticism does not eliminate the pantheistic view without this supporting demonstration. It is a restatement of what many pantheists willingly admit.

Fifth, some theists have argued that pantheism's God depends on creation. If creation is emanational, then the Creator is not the sovereign above the universe but is part of that universe. Again, this criticism does not negate the pantheistic system decisively. The pantheist admits, without damaging his system, that God depends on creation. He argues that this interdependency is in keeping with what we know of nature where ecosystems play an important role in the lives of all living things. Moreover, there is nothing conceptually inadequate about the interdependence of Creator and creation. This interdependence is logically possible and must be shown to be inadequate on independent grounds if this criticism is to be decisive.

Sixth, a more subtle attempt to render pantheism's position inadequate states that the pantheistic God is finite and infinite at the same time:

The idea that the world is a self-expression of God is incompatible with his infinity or self-existence. If God shares his being with the world he must be limited by it. Alternatively, if the world is (as it manifestly is and must be) contingent, and if it is a part of God, he cannot be necessary.[12]

If this criticism could be sustained, pantheism would seem to have a decisive problem. But to this criticism, as it is stated here, there are certain answers. To begin with, pantheism admits that, on the level of mere human thought, the existence of God seems contradictory. It must be remembered that the pantheist has built a system which ultimately transcends the logical distinctions of our categorical reasoning. Furthermore, this argument supposes that to be infinite is to be necessary in the Thomistic sense: that is, to be infinite one cannot change at all. But there is more than one sense to *infinite*. A pantheist could retort that God could be infinite in that he encompasses all that exists but that he is not therefore necessary in the Scholastic sense: God could be all there is and still change. To take another tack, pantheism need not necessarily admit that what we perceive as change really constitutes change. Pantheism could deny that things change in the ultimate sense and still be within its own guidelines.

Criticisms with Existential Value. The attempts we have already mentioned to reduce pantheism to incoherence seem to fail in one way or another. But there are arguments that do carry more weight. Such arguments may be absorbed into the pantheistic system without internal incoherency. But, as we will see, the implications of this process of absorption are rather difficult to live with, for these arguments appeal to strong intuitions that arise from daily existence.

One criticism of this existential variety argues that pantheism, by destroying individual existence, also destroys communication and love in this universe. There must be persons if there is to be communication. Very clearly we do experience interpersonal communication and love, so there must be individual persons. So goes the argument.[13]

Watts, however, is able to respond to this argument from the pantheistic viewpoint:

This argument cuts both ways because what the Christian says about the "Three in One and One in Three" relationship of the Trinity is almost exactly what the Hindu says about the "Many in One and One in Many" arrangement of the universe. If the latter makes love between the members unreal, so does the former.[14]

Watts' response carries some weight. It is true that one could have a unity of reality without destroying the possibility of experiencing communication between persons. To argue too strongly against Watts' concept at this point would undermine a concept which many Christians want to hold. In any case, Watts' view does not reduce to conceptual inadequacy at this point. Nevertheless, we can argue that Watts does not fully account for the vast quantity of our experiences which seem to presuppose separate individuals or personal centers of feeling, deciding and thinking.

This discussion, which is similar to a point which will be mentioned later, makes us ask how Watts can distinguish between the true experiences of unity or "cosmic consciousness" like Christ had and the illusory or misleading experiences of separate egos interacting and communicating with other egos. It is logically possible to hold simultaneously to the reality of ontological unity and the validity of interpersonal communication (Christians affirm this about the Trinity); however, many people do intuitively feel that pantheism cannot fully account for human experiences of interpersonal communication.

Second, a similar criticism has been advanced arguing that pantheism destroys human yearnings for religion by eliminating the possibility of worship. Religiously, says this argument, pantheism is strictly limited. While some versions may allow a quasi-mystical union with Reality as divine, salvation and prayer, for example, are precluded.[15]

But Watts answers this criticism as well. He admits that there are no personal relationships between God and individual people primarily because people do not exist as such. This criticism thus is not a criticism, but a statement of the pantheistic position. Furthermore, Watts explains any yearnings that men and women may have for religious fulfillment as the result of convention. Many pantheists and atheists live apparently contented lives without God; proving they need God for everyday living may be very difficult.

Watts' first response will be discussed in later sections. The undeniable existence of humans seems to be evidence from experience which pantheism cannot explain adequately. As for the second part of Watts' response (namely, that religious yearnings are the result of convention), it seems that Watts has failed to take seriously the statements of many who seek meaning which goes beyond human existence. Many Eastern religions hold that humanity's existential problem is ignorance. People simply do not realize who they are: they forget that they are really one with the universe. Salvation, therefore, is knowledge, consisting in a new apprehension of what has been the case all along: people must come to realize their unity with the universe and nothing more. But this analysis strikes many as inadequate. People seem to desire something more than this, because, it seems, they sense a need which is greater than the one identified by many Eastern thinkers, including Watts. To dismiss all desire for meaning which goes beyond human existence as conventional is to ignore a great deal of the evidence of human experience. In fact, many common people who live in Eastern societies (where pantheistic notions have greater influence) worship theistic deities of one sort or another. A primary example can be found in India where theistic Bhakti (devotion) cults include large numbers of adherents. Despite these facts, however, this criticism of Watts does not reduce his world view to conceptual incoherence, for Watts would simply argue that religious yearning ought to be eliminated. This criticism merely points out that pantheism seems to go against the grain of certain widely experienced and deeply felt intuitions about the place of humanity in this universe.

Third, another criticism in this category argues that this world view cannot (or does not) explain the reality of evil, suffering and death in the world. To say that suffering is illusory, say some, is not only philosophically inadequate, it is existentially superficial as well.[16]

In this case, Watts' response is twofold. First,

The constrictions and spasms of dying are felt as a frightful agony and a dreadfully serious occasion to the degree that one has been persuaded (a) that you arise in the world once and only once, and

(b) that to live is a moral compulsion and duty as well as an ingrained and ineradicable instinct.[17]
Second, because of this, Watts argues that honesty requires that we face life squarely. Continues Watts, we should not comfort the dying cancer patient with visions of a "pie-in-the-sky" heaven if in actual fact heaven is an illusion just like the suffering of cancer.

This facet of pantheism arouses particular existential distaste. If anything constitutes "acute awareness," the intense agony of severe physical suffering or mental anguish certainly does. But pantheists argue that the suffering of cancers, accidents and heart diseases are part of the great illusion, the cosmic game where the Lord is playing hide-and-seek in his *maya.* Aside from the fact that it flies in the face of a great deal of very intense human experience, this position is indeed existentially hollow. Again, this argument does not affect pantheism internally, but it does show how pantheism differs from what many people deeply feel to be the case.

Fourth, in a similar argument many have accused the pantheists of eliminating altogether the basis for the good/evil moral distinction. People consider themselves free agents and feel responsible for their conduct. They recognize a standard of morality which they must either incorporate into their lives or reject as superficial. But pantheism ignores altogether the basic moral categories.[18]

Watts could respond to this argument in several ways. Many argue for the moral distinction on the basis of the fact that people *feel* as though they are free agents. But pantheism has already rejected the feelings which arise from our consciousness of being individual egos. Nothing about the way we feel, says Watts, necessitates that morality be anything more than mere convention. Moreover, according to Watts, a "moral blindness which most theologians attribute to the pantheist is largely theoretical."[19] In practice, even Zen Buddhists follow a course of morality as a prelude to the *satori.* Finally, to take a different approach, accusing pantheism of blurring the good/evil distinction is only to reaffirm what the pantheists themselves assert. For the pantheist, conceptual distinctions are not part of reality as such but arise from our conventionally acquired modes of categorization and intellectualization. To argue that we must follow a good/evil distinction somewhere outside our humanity is merely to state the theistic position; it is not to criticize the pantheist.

The response to Watts' contentions in the area of morality parallels the last answer. While it is possible to hold that moral distinctions, because of their conceptual nature, are less than adequate expressions of reality, it is also true that this conclusion goes against the intuitions of many people. Does anyone really want to argue that the moral rules of the bee-game are no more or less important than those of the human-game? Does anyone really want to say that giving a job to an unemployed person at the expense of some personal profits is no better (morally speaking) than throwing him or her out on the street? Or does anyone really think that the atrocities committed against the Armenians and the Jews in our century are not in some way wrong? It seems that human beings intuit the true and valid place of moral distinctions in our world, despite the pantheists' arguments.

Pantheism's Major Problem. Pantheists will often admit the problems mentioned above as part of their system. Despite the existential repugnance that those admissions arouse, they do not necessarily reduce the pantheistic system to internal incoherence. These next arguments, however, present somewhat stronger criticisms of the pantheistic world view. Their primary thrust is that pantheism does not (and cannot) adequately explain human existence: how is it that human beings who think, feel and speak as we do ever came to be part of this universe?

Several arguments have been advanced in this regard. First, one attempt to reduce pantheism to a cul-de-sac holds that pantheism affirms the existence of finite beings in the very act of denying their existence. According to this argument, anyone who affirms the position of pantheism implicitly acknowledges that he speaks from a finite perspective. Unless there actually exists an intelligent source of the denial, the denial of the existence of human beings is impossible. At the same time the pantheist will not deny the validity of his own affirmation because this affirmation is believed to be true. The pantheist assumes and presupposes the existence of finite beings in the process of denying existence to such beings.

Watts could rejoin in several ways. The concept of the Trinity, which the Christian church would like to retain, provides a model by which one might possibly deny the existence of finite beings without defeating oneself. Many Christians would agree that before creation Christ could have denied the existence of finite beings without making either a self-defeating or false statement. Furthermore, many pantheists do not affirm from their finite existential perspective that finite beings do not exist. They argue that, while this statement cannot be communicated verbally (or even thought), it is not thereby rendered false. The mystical, intuitive experience of *satori* suggests through the feelings that human beings do not primarily exist as finite beings but as manifestations of God.

Several responses can be made to the pantheistic position at this point. It is logically possible to think of each human being as an incarnation of God based on the model that Christian theology has used in describing Jesus Christ. But saying that every human being is an incarnation like Jesus raises the question as to why the vast majority of human beings have never had the intense experience of "cosmic consciousness" that reveals one's ontological connection with God. In this and many other ways Christ seemed to live a life which was highly unusual.

As to the second point we shall comment at length later. To anticipate the form of the argument, it seems that the statement that finite individuals do not exist can be meaningful only if there is an intelligence of some sort making the statement. As Watts himself argued against the naturalist, if the whole "universe is meaningless, so is the statement that it is so. If this world is a vicious trap, so is its accuser, and the pot is calling the kettle black."[20] If the denial of real finite beings is to be meaningful, there must be some center of intelligence making that statement. This brings us back to asking the nature of these centers of intelligence. Buddhists in particular are concerned to deny *substantially* existing egos,[21] but this does not necessitate the denial of finite egos per se. Some centers of intelligence undeniably exist (whether or not it is proper to think of them in substantial terms), and it seems proper to ask the ontological status of these centers of intelligence. As we mentioned above, the majority of human beings have never had the experience of "cosmic consciousness," and it seems intuitively clear to them that they are not one with the universe. Many may seem to enjoy communion with ultimate reality, perhaps, but most do not seem to experience union.

Second, a more recent attempt to discredit pantheism is found in the argument that pantheism does not justify its own assumption of an unusual concept or understanding of being (that which exists). An ancient Greek philosopher named Parmenides had argued for a strict monism or pantheism by assuming what has been called a univocal concept of being, which means that beings must be univocal or exactly the same. In this kind of a view, unless something is exactly the same as being itself, then it cannot really exist. According to this concept of being, it is impossible for two beings to be similar (in that they are both beings) and yet distinct (in that they are different beings). If this is true, then what appear to be two beings would either be one and the same being, or only one could really be a being and the other would have to be nonbeing or not real. The result in either case, therefore, is a pantheism where all of reality is ontologically related. It seems that Parmenides did not seriously consider the analogical concept of being wherein different beings could be similar in that they are all beings, but different in other respects. If he had considered the possibility of a number of similar but distinct beings, Parmenides would not have been forced to accept a monism. According to this objection, then, a basic metaphysical assumption of pantheism is a univocal concept of being which leads to circular reasoning and numerous conceptual difficulties.[22]

Watts might have responded in this way. Pantheism can say that this criticism ignores the fact that all metaphysical world views must take some concept of being as a starting point or they will never get off the ground. Further, he could retort that this criticism is valid only if the pantheist argues that the univocal concept of being is the *only* possible alternative. Then a nonpantheist could respond that an analogical concept of being is clearly a possible option. But because Watts feels little compulsion to find the Truth (because, in his view, the heaven/hell alternative is far-fetched and less than serious), he wants only to find a *possible* explanation for our universe. In this way the burden of proof could be shifted to the nonpantheist.

Despite these responses, the basic criticism carries some weight. The univocal concept of being assumed by pantheism gets Watts into conceptual difficulty. At one point Watts admits that the pantheistic world view has enormous paradoxes and antinomies at its heart. For example, if our union with God is to be perfect, then it must be an intimate and inseparable kind of union. But if God is really to be God, he must be infinitely above and beyond the universe. Again, if God is the source of creative power and life, he cannot be less than a person. But if he is the ultimate reality, then he must be free from the mutability and limitation of finite personality as we know it. In line with his general rejection of logic, Watts blames these paradoxical elements on the conceptual, logical modes of thought.[23] But it seems rather that an unfounded assumption of the univocal concept of being, and the implicit rejection of the analogous concept where several beings can be alike in some ways but different in others, was the source of the paradoxes.

God, for example, could be like human beings in that he is a person who can relate and commune with other persons. He could be different, however, in that his personhood would not be limited as is ours. Personhood per se is not what causes all human limitation, and thus it is possible to be personal without having all the limitations of human existence. This is precisely what theists claim about God: God is personal yet not limited like humans. Thus while every world view must take some concept of being as a starting point, it seems that the concept of analogous being avoids the kind of paradoxes that plague Watts' assumption.

Third, some critics have argued that pantheism does not satisfactorily explain our experience as individual, finite egos. Owen argues, "Pantheism fails to explain our awareness of distinctness and autonomy in things and persons. Our total experience of both personal and sub-personal entities is pervaded by the conviction that each is an independent form of existence."[24]

Watts would probably respond to this criticism in this way. For Christians there remains the problem of Jesus, whom Christianity holds to be one with the Father. There can be no doubt, according to Watts, that he experienced both an awareness of distinction and an obvious consciousness of divine closeness or oneness. Moreover, Watts does explain his assertion that our experience as individuals is illusory. Briefly, according to Watts, the ego-illusion arose because God, in the farthest reaches of his game of hide-and-seek, simply forgot who he was. Once he remembers who he is (as he does in the mystical experience of "cosmic consciousness") there is no problem in understanding how the sensation of individual selfhood is a total illusion. We are God's alter egos playing the black side of the cosmic chess game while he plays the white.

But this line of explanation by Watts strikes many as less than satisfactory. While there exists no logical problem with thinking of human beings as incarnations much like Jesus Christ, there remains the problem of the vast accumulation of the experience of individual identity felt by persons in every culture and at every time. When Watts explains human existence as God playing the cosmic chess match, he falls short of providing a theory which explains all the evidence of human experience. If plausibility is a logical notion (and it is when Watts uses it to judge other world views or religions), then there must be a meaningful reason for rejecting the majority of experiential evidence in favor of the evidence accumulated in the mystical experience. To consider the evidence from a mystical experience of oneness and unity to be valid and the evidence from the more ordinary experience of separateness and community to be invalid simply because that is how the world view says it should be is to let the conclusion determine the evidence and not the other way around. To say that God is playing two sides of the cosmic chess match does give us an internally coherent way of understanding the pantheistic world view, but it does not give any evidence on its behalf.

Watts' other illustration of God's *maya* does no better. To offer the game of celestial hide-and-seek as the final explanation of all individual existence, including its modes of thinking, feeling and speaking, its joys and sorrows, its experiences of communication and love (ad infinitum) seems inadequate. It is hard to imagine that all human experience could be so simply and easily explained. There must be more reason to reject the testimony of everyday living than simply that this testimony contradicts the pantheistic world view.

Criticisms of Watts' View of Christianity
The second major section of this discussion concerns Watts' view of the relationship between pantheism and Christianity. By his own admission, his early attempts to synthesize

these two systems of thought were inadequate, and in his later work Watts came to realize the mutually exclusive natures of these two systems of faith.

It should be kept in mind that to hold that two statements from two different systems contradict one another is implicitly to agree to the validity of logic. There can be no contradictions without logic. Therefore, this admission by Watts seems to imply both the necessity of deciding between several (at least two) ways of viewing reality and the validity of using logic in that choice.

The Philosophia Perennis. The *Philosophia Perennis*, according to Aldous Huxley, consists of a common core of intuition among mystics of all ages that recognizes a divine reality within the world as we sensibly perceive it.[25] To the end of his life, Watts seemed to feel that the *Philosophia Perennis* provided a valid position.[26] He wrote unequivocally, "The fact of a given union with God, given without respect to virtue or holiness, has been the central and secret joy of many a mystic, Christian and non-Christian, in all times and places."[27]

But the argument that there exists a unified system of belief supported by the mystical experiences of all cultures at all times is open to question. The most important problem that undermines the *Philosophia Perennis* is the breadth of the theological and philosophical assertions made by those persons who have supposedly supported their world views by means of a single mystical epistemology. On closer examination there are really many differences in the systems supported by mysticism, and the *Philosophia Perennis* must explain how they can all mean one and the same thing. As William James noted after his careful study of mystical experiences, "So many men, so many minds: I imagine that these experiences can be as infinitely varied as are the idiosyncrasies of the individuals."[28]

Another problem is closely related to this objection: mystical experience is not only irreducible to one common core of truth, but there seems to be no way to reconcile all the diversified assertions of the various mystics at a level where a world view can be supported. Any common content, argue many, seems to appear at a level of generality which is too diluted to provide epistemological support to any world view, much less a specific religion. For mystical experience to gain the necessary consistency required by any cognitively meaningful claim to knowledge, its content must usually be generalized to such an extent that the results are disappointing to the partisans of each particular world view.[29]

Interestingly enough, the chief proponent of the *Philosophia Perennis*, Aldous Huxley himself, made statements on his deathbed which seem to support this line of thinking. As Huxley spoke from his bed under the influence of a sedative drug, his wife tape-recorded his comments. He thought that perhaps he had reached the state of timeless bliss called by the Tibetan Buddhists the "Clear Light of the Void." But the recording apparently showed that mystical intuitions do not always provide even personal, psychological certitude. He said,

This whole thing has been very strange because in a way it was very good–but in a way it was absolutely terrifying, showing that when one thinks one's got beyond oneself, one hasn't. . . . I began with this marvelous sense of this cosmic gift, and then ended up with a rueful sense that one can be deceived. . . . It was an insight, but at the same time the most dangerous of errors . . . inasmuch as one was worshipping oneself.[30]

Huxley apparently admitted that a mystical epistemology can at times be problematic.

Watts himself came to realize that accepting the *Philosophia Perennis* with its mystical epistemology (logically) means that one must reject Christianity as it is traditionally understood. Watts had made three major attempts to bring Christianity and pantheism into a synthesis.[31] But these attempts were unsatisfying. Watts found no evidence that Christianity has ever been aware of itself as one form among several, all of which reduce to a common meaning. Christianity has always been a contentious faith which requires total commitment to Christ as a unique Incarnation and revelation of God. Watts felt that his early discussions had failed to take account of Christianity's "uncompromising, ornery, militant, rigorous, imperious, and invincibly self-righteous" aspects.[32] As Watts finally came to agree, Christianity presupposes a world view which contradicts that of pantheism.

Watts' Rejection of Christianity. Realizing the need for a choice between pantheism and the world view presupposed by Christianity is but half the battle. Next one must determine the grounds on which to make that decision. Watts was right to realize that the facets of Christianity which were objectionable to him could not be shrugged off as temporary or incidental errors. For this reason, Watts went on to argue that Christianity was unliveable and ought to be rejected.[33]

But the reasoning behind this conclusion left something to be desired. At times, for example, Watts raised criticisms that were somewhat abusive. After presenting his unified view of reality, he mused,

Christians, who so often affect prickly and astringent attitudes, may cluck and pish-tush that this is all very imprecise, vague, woolly, and sentimental. But in the harsh clacking of their disciplined voices, their accurate distinctions, and precise calculations, I hear the rattle of rifle bolts and the clicking of heels. "Like a mighty army moves the Church of God." But this is no way for a gentle-man.[34]

Another more serious objection should be made to Watts' rather free use of the Bible. To argue that Watts must interpret the Bible or any other religious literature in a particularly Christian fashion would not in itself be a criticism. However, if Watts takes the context of biblical passages with perfect seriousness in certain cases but ignores the context at other times, we have good reason to complain. To take one example, Watts takes the saying of Jesus, "If therefore thine eye be single, thy whole body shall be full of light" (Mt. 6:22, KJV), as an expression of the Buddhist concept of a Third Eye which shows that life is nondualistic.[35] But such an interpretation of the passage clearly seems to take the statement of Jesus out of its original context which concerns single-minded devotion to God. With such hermeneutical liberties the Bible can be made to support almost anything.

Another inadequate facet of Watts' criticism of Christianity is his willingness to hold up the crude imagery of more naive believers to ridicule. Such criticisms often do not affect the more sophisticated concepts of the theologians who support a particular world view. Watts' basic reason for rejecting the theistic model, according to his own testimony, is the crude imagery of God as an Oriental potentate with his torture chamber called hell. He even admits at one point, "I am not, of course, speaking of God as conceived by the most subtle Jewish, Christian, and Islamic theologians, but of the popular image. For it is the vivid image rather than the tenuous concept which has the greater influence on common sense."[36] If Watts admits to attacking the "popular image," it does not seem that this in itself could really raise problems with the theistic world view in principle, at least as it has been conceived through history by intelligent theologians. Certainly the image of Oriental monarchs is not crucial to Christian theism. To raise a fuss about it is not to render the theistic model implausible but merely to encourage the tendency toward greater sophistication.

Despite the inadequacy of Watts' arguments against Christianity, it is important to emphasize the point at which Watts' view coincides with Christianity. He agrees that pantheism and Christianity are mutually exclusive systems which must ultimately be surrendered to arbitration. Watts finally made his choice and concluded that our feeling of being solitary visitors in this universe is in "flat contradiction" to everything we know via modern science about humanity's relationship to its environment.[37] This conclusion shows once again Watts' implicit acceptance of logic and even seems to imply that evidence for choosing between world views is not entirely beyond the experiences of ordinary consciousness, but can be found in the observations of the sciences as well as in the experiences of the mystic.

Criticisms of Mystical Epistemology

Our third area of discussion centers on Watts' epistemology which is based on mystical intuition. There are several reasons why mysticism fails to provide evidence for meaningful knowledge about reality.

The Process of Mysticism. Mystical epistemology encounters problems at several points. Most fundamentally, it is possible to argue that all experience goes through the grid of the mind as it is apprehended, even in the most immediate form. Many have argued that experience, whether sensory, emotional, rational or mystical, passes through the mind and is interpreted by it: there is no such thing as "raw experience."[38] For example, most mystics tend to maintain theories about reality which they already believed before their mystical experience or at least to express their experiences in categories with which they and their contemporaries were familiar. This seems to indicate the highly influential role played by the notions which are already in the mind before the mystical experience is encountered. Significant in this regard is the testimony of the modern Hindu philosopher, Radhakrishnan: "Religious experience is not the pure unvarnished presentment of the real in itself, but is the presentment of the real already influenced by the ideas and prepossessions of the perceiving mind."[39] Clearly the burden of proof lies with one who argues that mystical experience can indeed be an unaffected, immediate, "pure" apprehension of what is.

Another problem lies in the nature of psychological certitude. William James concluded from his study that the mystical experience may carry a great deal of weight for the mystic himself.[40] But the question remains whether this type of certitude is sufficient to insure the attainment of "knowledge." In a court of law, for example, the witness who can assert with great vigor, "*I am sure* the accused is guilty," is of little value to the prosecution without a response to the question as to *why* he or she thinks the accused is guilty.[41] It is not sufficient for the witness simply to say, "I *feel* sure." Those deciding the case will demand that the witness provide a description of the experience that led to the belief that the accused is guilty. If the witness can say something like, "I heard the victim scream and saw the accused running from the scene of the crime with gun in hand," then the question as to why the accused is believed to be guilty will have been answered in a satisfactory manner. But if the witness says that he or she has never liked the accused because the accused is a bully, the court will never convict the accused. As in this illustration, we always demand more than mere psychological certainty whenever a question of any importance is being decided.

Furthermore, if another witness can give evidence that the accused was present at another location at the time of the crime, the first witness's testimony will be held up to question. If seven reputable witnesses can attest the fact that the accused was present at another location at the time of the crime, and only one witness claims to have seen the accused at the scene of the crime, then those in the court will tend to conclude that the one witness has made a mistake and the defense will try to attribute that error to some mitigating circumstance (such as poor lighting conditions, for example). If, however, several witnesses can positively identify the accused as the one who committed the crime, then the court will be much more likely to convict. In general terms, whenever a large number of individuals can all agree as to what they experienced, the chances that one individual's personal prejudices, perceptual shortcomings or other idiosyncracies will cause errors to arise are greatly decreased (though not necessarily eliminated). This element of "intersubjective verifiability," which means that several subjects or persons can all confirm the validity of a certain experience despite their varied backgrounds, is essential to an epistemology which seeks to overcome the possibilities that a particular individual might be deluded, mistaken or confused.

Mystical experience suffers because it is a very private affair, and this limits the possibilities of intersubjective verification. Desire for this sort of intersubjective confirmation seems to lie behind the popularity of the *Philosophia Perennis:* if all mystics have an experience which has clearly similar characteristics and conclusions, then an element of intersubjective verification can be attained. But, as we have argued, the level of agreement among various mystics is so small as to be disappointing to the adherents of one particular world view. Without confirmation by others, the possibility for error rises markedly so that, as Martin Buber said in his famous line, we can always wonder whether we are being addressed by the Absolute or by one of his apes.[42] Mystical experience, by itself, seems to lack the possibility for intersubjective confirmation that would begin to overcome the problems inherent in purely private experience.

Further, mystical experience does not always provide even psychological certitude. As useless as such certainty is (by itself) in deciding between world views, it is not clear that even it can always be attained in mystical experience. As we noted before, Huxley's final words admitted that his mystical experience did not necessarily yield personal, psychological certitude. According to one commentator, Huxley realized that what he had taken to be transcendent Wisdom was a great deal more like Jung's concept of "positive inflation" in which one ends up doing no more than worshiping oneself.[43] There seems to be no way to eliminate the possibility that the process of a mystical, intuitional epistemology leads to error at least some of the time.

A mystic might respond, however, by arguing that mystical experience could fail to give certitude part of the time and still be valid at other times. After all, goes this response, the ordinary conscious experience upon which many individuals base their world views does not always provide certainty but sometimes leads to error. Yet those who put confidence in the experiences of ordinary consciousness do not, because of occasional error, discount the evidence of ordinary consciousness altogether.

While this is a reasonable response, there are several factors which mitigate its significance. Mystical experience is allegedly immediate and intuitive in contrast to ordinary experience which is mediated through the senses and the mind, and is discursive or nonintuitive. If an error arises in a particular empirical argument, the source of the error can be found, for there are (in principle as well as in fact) places where errors can arise. One could blame an error on the process of observation which was muddied either by perceptual difficulties or prejudiced by presupposed opinions. Likewise, the process of reasoning may have been fouled by some logical fallacy. But mystical epistemologies have no place for error in principle (although there are errors in fact if mystics come up with contrary views of reality). For this reason, if several mystics disagree as to the significance of their experience, the consequences are worse than if several empiricists disagree. If a mystic argues that the mystical experience can be wrong part of the time and still valid the rest of the time, he raises the difficult problem of finding a criterion which will distinguish between valid and invalid mystical experiences. To make this distinction strictly on the basis of mystical intuition seems rather difficult, for it seems the contrast will be logical and thus distasteful to many mystics.

Similarly, there remains for the mystic the problem of how to distinguish between experience of ordinary consciousness and that of mystical intuition. Watts had a theoretical answer prepared for this very problem. He once argued that while humanity's experience is generally misleading, the source of true knowledge is still experience. There must therefore be some measure or criterion by which to determine which experience is valid and which is illusory. Watts answered that mystical intuition "involves a far more acute awareness of the plain evidences of the sense than is usual."[44] But far from solving the problem, this answer at best moves the question back one step, for it is still possible to ask what "acute awareness" means and to question whether it would ever be possible for one to know just when he or she was being struck by it, if it were ever to come. And like before, the mystic must face the fact that even if these questions could be solved, the answers would be rational and intellectual, and the chances for an immediate, uncontaminated mystical experience are thereby decreased.

Watts argued that "acute awareness" was not a retreat into a private and thus relative world of its own simply because "its entire concern is to transcend subjectivity, so that man may 'wake up' to the world which is concrete and actual, as distinct from that which is purely abstract and conceptual."[45] Watts wants us to apprehend the *real* world, as opposed to the world as we sensibly perceive it. But here another problem arises. How can an ineffable experience which cannot be expressed to another human, no matter how acute, ever become more than a subjective and private affair? If communication is precluded (and most mystics agree that it is), then one can never really know what others are thinking or feeling, and public experience becomes impossible. If supposedly similar experiences (we would never really know if they were similar) felt by different individuals cannot be compared, then there can be no intersubjective verification. In the analogy of the courtroom, if there is only one witness to any given piece of information, then the case of the prosecution will never be very strong. Strong testimony is achieved when several people can agree that they have had experiences which point to the same conclusion. At least in principle, if not in actual fact, evidence must be open to evaluation by many people if it is to count as evidence.

Closely related to the problem of the private and ineffable nature of mystical experience is the question as to whether the mystic ever properly expresses what he has privately experienced. Even though some have argued that the mystic may be able to speak *of* his experience at a later time (though he cannot speak during the experience), one can still question the veracity of the report.[46] Has the experience per se (ignoring for the moment the thorny question of proper interpretation) been correctly reported? It seems unlikely that a mystic could ever assure someone else that his report is correct. Even if his report were correct, demonstration of that fact seems nearly impossible.[47]

The Results of Mysticism. The process of mystical experience poses difficulties for the mystic, but the fact that the mystical epistemology can and does result in systems of widely differing varieties also presents problems. Eastern mystical pantheists, anthropomorphic Spanish saints and neoplatonic Christians all expound their mystical revelations primarily in the terms of the doctrinal system or world view which they respectively represent.[48] Such diversity in the results of mystical experiences led James to assert that mystics have "no right . . . to invoke its prestige as distinctively in favor of any specific belief, such as that in absolute idealism, or in the absolute monistic identity, or in the absolute goodness of the world."[49]

This criticism leads to another similar question. As we pointed out in our discussion of the *Philosophia Perennis*, the common "core" of truth which can be found among the assertions of all mystics is quite small.[50] Whenever the metaphysical assertions that have been supported by an appeal to mystical experience are compared, the least common denominator is so small and generalized that it is rather disappointing to anyone who would use it as a basis for the choice between world views that we have found to be necessary.[51]

Of course, mystics can claim that their knowledge is ineffable (often because conceptual differences are inconsequential). Watts makes such claims, affirming that anything the dualistically trained mind attempts to do would go wrong, simply because one cannot stand outside the world without getting into that paradoxical situation of thinking about thinking, thinking about thinking about thinking, ad infinitum. Watts wants a knowledge of "unknowing" which is typical of many who claim the mystical epistemology. They assert that the truth they seek lies beyond categorical knowledge; this helps them avoid the criticism that the content of mystical intuition is too limited to be worthwhile. The knowledge of "unknowing" can envelop inconsistent statements without problem, thus broadening the content of mystical experience.[52]

But this move creates problems. The illustration of the boat and the river (the boat of discursive reasoning and rationality helps one cross the river to the opposite bank where truth beyond intellectualization lies) has at its heart a basic difficulty. It can be argued that limiting knowledge within a certain sphere is impossible because in order to separate the known from the unknown one must have already done what is affirmed to be impossible: one must know the unknowable.[53] Quite clearly, we cannot draw a boundary unless we can see the other side. The attempt to circumscribe all knowledge and then to make meaningful assertions about something which exists outside the circle is self-defeating. The claim to "know" something which is beyond knowledge either turns on and defeats itself, or it uses *know* in a highly unusual (perhaps even meaningless) fashion.

The mystic puts himself into such a double-bind the moment he rejects or relaxes the laws of logic. As soon as we try to deny the validity of logic, we realize that we are using logic in the process. These laws are necessary to our thinking and speaking: undeniably, making sense of our experience presupposes logic.

This is not to say that human beings cannot have an experience which goes beyond the capabilities of human thought, for there are experiences which do just this. Aesthetic experiences like listening to music, for example, do not always lend themselves to complete description. But then, aesthetic experiences do not give us information about the way things are either. A totally inexplicable pain in one's hand, to take another example, also may resist the categorizations of human thought and language. But such an experience "makes no sense"; if it cannot be attributed to some cause or explained under some general rule concerning a type of pain in the hand, the experience must finally be discarded as a meaningless experience. Such experiences do not contribute anything to our understanding of the universe or to the process of making sense out of finite human existence.

Summary
We conclude this chapter of criticism with several summary statements. First, in our discussion of the traditional theistic criticisms of pantheism, we found that pantheism as an ontological and metaphysical world view remains difficult to criticize. Some of the critiques which have been advanced, in fact, have exhibited a circularity which has sometimes left pantheism standing quite unaffected. Pantheism, as a world view, is internally consistent, existentially useful and, granted its presuppositions, coherent.

One difficulty with the pantheistic world view is its inability to explain the human experience of existence as finite egos. If one assumes the pantheistic view of human existence a priori, then it is not difficult to make the system fit together coherently, for any evidence which contradicts the system's beliefs can be explained as invalid. But if one starts with the overwhelming forcefulness of ordinary human consciousness, it does not seem that many would reach the conclusion that human existence is merely illusion. For Watts to offer God's cosmic game of hide-and-seek or the celestial chess match as the explanation of the primary evidence of centuries of human experience seems inadequate. Watts does not explain human existence; he explains it away.

Second, Watts (rightly) stresses in his later work the mutually exclusive nature of Christianity (as it is traditionally understood) and pantheism as he understood it. It is most important to remember that Christianity remains incurably theistic, rightly or wrongly, and the choice for or against Christianity must be made with that stubborn fact in mind. Thus the authority of Christian mystics cannot be used to support pantheism, for their conclusions differ from those of Huxley, Suzuki and Watts.

Third, despite Watts' complaints about theism's attempts to fixate the flux of the world process, the laws of logic are undeniably the modes of our speaking and thinking. Any attempt to deny the validity of logic must use logic in its denial, and thus the denial turns on and defeats itself. According to Watts, life is understandable and meaningful only if it is pressed into an arbitrary framework of rigid laws. But this goal can never be reached: it is the attempt to fixate the flux.[54] In response, we admit that if life and logic have nothing in common, then we should not seek to understand life. But the problem with Watts at this point is twofold. On the one hand, as we stated, it is not possible to meaningfully deny that logic applies to this universe. And on the other hand, even if it were possible, it is still important to ask what sort of sense we are to make of the many writings of Watts and other mystical pantheists if they have nothing to do with logic.

Fourth, we as human beings do not think, speak or know anything about a universe which is not grounded on the laws of logic. Defending this point will be the purpose of the final chapter where we will argue that all attempts to deny the laws of logic in our modes of speech and thought result in either self-defeat or meaninglessness. If this is a pantheistic universe, it is impossible to know it to be so, and Watts (like other pantheists) must explain to us once again why and how human beings came to think and speak as they do. But this is precisely the problem. Watts cannot eliminate all experience as false and conventional because his own epistemology depends heavily on experience as the source of knowledge. But neither can he differentiate between a valid mystical experience and an invalid conventional experience (i.e., our experience of being finite individuals), for logical distinctions are not ultimately valid. What is more, any attempt at such a distinction would be a rational enterprise and thus on Watts' system it would be doomed from the start. It does not seem that Watts can decisively eliminate the overwhelming evidence experienced by human beings in many cultures and at many times which suggests that we do indeed exist as finite individuals.

6

A
FINAL
APOLOGY

While a universe which transcends our modes of thinking and speaking always remains a logical possibility, a claim to "know" something beyond these modes does produce grave difficulties. When Watts claims to "know" his pantheistic position to be the case, he argues that God (or ultimate reality) is unknowable by intellectual processes because he (it) is indescribable and ineffable; according to this view meaningful predication of God is impossible. This does not mean that God is absolutely unknowable, but simply that he is unknowable by thought: God can still be known by an intuitive experience or by an immediate consciousness of union with God through a primarily moral rather than intellectual process.[1]

The Basic Dilemma
Making the claim, "God is unknowable by intellection," presents a difficult problem. There are only two possible ways in which such a claim could be understood: such an affirmation could be a theory which is meant by the affirmer to apply

meaningfully to God or it might be meaningless, something which is meant to apply meaningfully to nothing in particular. This poses a dilemma for the mystic. On the one hand, if "God is unknowable by intellection" is meant to apply to God, then the claim turns back on itself. If nothing about God is knowable, then one obviously cannot know that "God is unknowable by intellection." If "reality is unknowable by intellection" is a theory about reality to the effect that theories about reality are impossible, then it turns on and defeats itself. No argument against the possibility of knowing God through the intellectual use of experience can be sustained, for the conclusion would be a theory about God which purports to be intellectually knowable. The mystics' objection to ordinary intellectual reasoning is itself a theory and thus, on the mystics' own criterion, can never be known as true. In sum, the pantheist, when he appeals to mystical epistemology, assumes and uses the laws of logic in the very process of denying their validity, and therefore faces self-defeat whenever he makes an allegedly meaningful affirmation.

A mystic could object that many claims which deny the possibility of intellectually knowing and describing certain experiences are not only meaningful but true. For example, the sentence, "A symphony cannot be understood by the intellect," would not be either self-defeating or meaningless, even though it denies the validity of intellectual knowing and describing within the realm of musical experience. In response, it must be noted that statements which deny the validity of intellection within a limited sphere are meaningful. "A symphony cannot be understood by the intellect". does not imply the denial of *all* statements which truly describe what exists, and therefore it can be both meaningful and true. To say that an experience of music cannot be understood by intellection is not to say anything about the process of making that statement, and thus it does not defeat itself. Only assertions which deny the possibility of *all* meaningful assertions have the fatal problem of defeating themselves.

On the other hand, it may be the case that the statement, "God cannot be known by intellection," is a statement which is not actually meant to apply to God. That is, this assertion may not really be meant as a theory about God. In this case, the mystics' objections to normal intellectual and experiential knowing do not apply to God and reality, which seems to imply that they can safely be ignored. Jumbled thought, unintelligent noises and stray marks on paper do not constitute meaningful objections to the claims of nonmystics to know something about what is.[2] In sum, if all meaningful human communication, thought and knowledge are based on the laws of logic, then it can be argued that the mystic who repudiates logic knows nothing meaningful about reality.

Of course, the mystic may object that he knows one proposition which applies literally and meaningfully to what is, namely, "No statements besides this one can apply literally to reality." Paul Tillich made a similar move under pressure of criticisms which demonstrated that if *all* statements are symbolic in their application, then the system reduces to meaninglessness. Tillich thus rescued his position by arguing that there is indeed one, though only one, statement which is not symbolic in its description of God. According to his admission, "God is the Ground of Being" became the one nonsymbolic statement.

While such a move could save the system, it also has unhappy repercussions for the mystic, for if one statement or theory literally applies to reality, then Pandora's box has been opened, and the mystic must now explain how and why every other statement or theory fails to apply meaningfully to reality. The mystic must also show why it is this one statement and not some other which is the one statement that applies literally. These tasks seem doomed from the start if for no other reason than that the mystic must pass through a potentially infinite series in order to falsify the claim that other statements and theories do indeed apply to reality. That is, the theory dies the death of a thousand qualifications. Thus while such medicine may save the life of a mystic's theory temporarily, its side effects may ultimately kill the hypothesis.

Reactions to the Dilemma

This dilemma is particularly ruthless, even though mystics do not always consciously face its full fury. But one group of mystics, the Zen masters of China and Japan, does seem to have felt intuitively the force of this dilemma. It seems possible that it is because of this dilemma that Zen masters do not assert the self-defeating propositions that propose meaningfully that meaningful affirmations about reality are impossible. Instead, as many stories relate, Zen masters often answer disciples' queries with nonsensical responses. Once, for example, the following exchange passed between an old master and an uninitiated novice:

"What is the Tao (i.e., God, reality)?"

"Walk on!"

"I have just come to this monastery; please give me some instruction."

"Have you finished your breakfast?"

"Yes."

"Then wash your dishes."[3]

Despite the overt rejection of statements about ultimate reality, Zen has shown that it somehow implicitly passes cognitive content of some sort down through the generations of masters and disciples. Zen claims that the intuitive *satori* can be induced strictly by the *koan*. But it seems that the *koan* would not have propagated Zen teaching were it not for the context in which the *koan* is administered. Without this context, which implicitly passes on some sort of content (e.g., if the *koan* were given in Rome, in Middletown, U.S.A., or in the middle of the Amazon jungle), it seems clear that a kick in the shins would never induce *satori*. Thus while Zen masters appear to avoid this dilemma by their mutism, they actually seem to fall into it in at least two ways: they think the content which cannot be spoken (a process which is also self-defeating) and they implicitly and nonverbally express minimal cognitive content by way of the context or environment that accompanies the administration of the *koan.*

Contemporary writers have displayed differing reactions to this dilemma. D. T. Suzuki, whose writings are a primary reason for the popularity of Zen in the West, admitted that one of the horns of the dilemma is a valid description of the actual state of affairs. When two monks of differing eras were asked if a great, cosmic fire destroys the universe at the end of time, one answered yes and the other no. Suzuki commented on this apparent contradiction by asserting that there is no need for alarm, for Zen can embody both answers with perfect consistency. This is because, in his words, "Zen would serenely go its own way without at all heeding such criticisms. Because Zen's first concern is about its experience and not its modes of expression." For Suzuki, expressions often include paradoxes, ambiguities and contradictions, but those "who have a genuine Zen experience will at once recognize in spite of superficial discrepencies what is true and what is not."[4] How this could be the case is not entirely clear; if we can only know and think in terms of logic and if reality does not have anything to do with logic, then knowing anything about reality seems hopeless.

Alan Watts chooses rather to take the other horn of the dilemma. Repeatedly in Watts' writings there appears the admission that "Reality, God, the Eternal Now, is entirely beyond speech and understanding and attainment."[5] He writes that theology seeks "the God which traditional doctrine calls the boundless, formless, infinite, eternal, undivided, and unchanging Reality," but the problem with theology is that "the Absolute [is] behind the relative, the Meaning [is] behind the thoughts and words."[6] Again, *because God is the maker of all sensible and intelligible things, he himself can neither be sensed nor known. As transcendent, he can never be the object of experience or knowledge, and, conversely, no particular experience or state of mind can be the immediate knowledge of God.*[7]

Clearly, Watts holds that the modes of thought and speech which we as humans use (i.e., the modes with which we undeniably think and speak) are meaningless.

Interestingly, Watts at one point gives his rationale for asserting that theological and dogmatic statements, as well as other sorts of statements which use logic, are meaningless. The mystic does not make dogmatic statements about what really exists because he knows that they "cannot describe his experience exactly." Like the poet, his statements are not literal and exact, but are figurative and metaphorical. He makes statements (if at all) only because there "is no other language available and appropriate." Just as it is absurd to "imagine that the poet really means that his beloved has cherries for lips and raven's wings for hair" so it is ridiculous to take the statements of the mystic in a literal sense.[8]

Watts apparently did not see that there are two alternative methods of applying statements to a subject. Watts assumes that a statement must either be univocally or literally applicable to reality or not applicable at all. Theological and dogmatic statements obviously cannot be univocally or literally ascribed to God (even theists admit this point), and therefore Watts concludes that dogmatic statements cannot be ascribed at all. Watts unfortunately ignores the second possibility (the alternative defended meaningfully by theists and others) that statements can be metaphorically or analogically applied to subjects. No one would argue that the poet's lover did indeed have cherries for lips, but to deny that her lips were at all *like* cherries in any respect seems rather incredible. Human beings often use analogy and metaphor to understand each other rather successfully. Similarly, theists use this method of description to make meaningful assertions about God.

Of course, this discussion does not answer why Watts seems to be making dogmatic statements himself. After all, he published about twenty-five books full of statements of all sorts which purport to be truly applicable to reality. Watts alluded to this problem in the prefaces of two of his books. In one he asserted, "If, then, I sometimes make statements in an authoritative and dogmatic manner, it is for the sake of clarity rather than from the desire to pose as an oracle."[9] This answer leaves the question in a cloud of ambiguity: does he or does he not mean for his statements to apply to reality?

A further question comes to mind during such a discussion. If Watts did not mean to apply his dogmatic statements to reality because he felt that all such assertions are by their very nature impossible to ascribe to reality, then why did he go about writing philosophy at all? What possible motivation could there be to fill more than twenty-five books with statements which do not really mean anything? Interestingly, in what seems to be an admission of the meaninglessness of his own work, Watts answered this very question:

If, then, I am not saying that you ought to awaken from the ego-illusion and help save the world from disaster, why The Book? Why not sit back and let things take their course? Simply that it is part of "things taking their course" that I write. As a human being it is just my nature to enjoy and share philosophy. I do this in the same way that some birds are eagles and some doves, some flowers lilies and some roses. I realize, too, that the less I preach, the more likely I am to be heard.[10]

If this notion is to be taken with any seriousness, the implications for daily life seem rather momentous. What does life mean? A Zen writer, Christmas Humphreys, faced this question and concluded that if there is "a washing-up to be finished, or a war to be won; let them be done." Naturally, emotions may get out of hand if we jump feet first into all our activities. But we need not repress them; if our emotions run high, then "use them, develop them, express the highest in you by their means." We should "take them for a run" at times and not be afraid to "sing, shout, get excited, whether with great beauty, a local football match or, best of all, great fun." This means we can compete in "sport or trade or politics, so long as [we] do not imagine that it matters in the least who wins." The only important part of such exercise is "the excitement itself, the letting off of steam.... The game, whether of football, national politics, or international war, has no intrinsic validity."[11]

In sum, while it is always logically possible that we live in a pantheistic universe, Watts' world view has difficulties in making sense of our existence. Not only is Watts unable to explain human existence with its sensations of finite individuality, he has built a system which cannot be meaningfully affirmed. It is always logically possible that there is more to "the universe than normal experience can understand or comprehend,"[12] but if this universe is pantheistic, there remains the thorny problem of how and why human beings came to exist, speak, think and feel as they do. Watts cannot eliminate all experience as false and conventional because his knowledge is based on experience. Neither can he differentiate between valid mystical experience and conventional pseudoexperience (i.e., our experience of finite existence) because that distinction would be a rational one. It seems that a mystical pantheism has difficulty eliminating the overwhelming experience of being a finite ego from the realm of valid experience.

As we have stated before, however, the pantheist himself might not be convinced by such argumentation. As D. T. Suzuki once wrote,

How can Zen permit the contradiction and continue the claim for its consistent teaching, one may ask. But Zen would serenely go its own way without at all heeding such a criticism. Because Zen's first concern is about its experience and not its modes of expression. The latter allow a great deal of variation, including paradoxes, contradictions, and ambiguities. According to Zen, the question of "is-ness" ... is settled only by innerly experiencing it and not by merely arguing about it or by linguistically appealing to dialectical subtleties.[13]

With this understanding of logical incoherencies, any world view becomes impossible to criticize. If the adherents of a particular world view admit that their view of reality is unconcerned with such logical problems, then they take the wind out of the critics' sails, so to speak. Logical criticisms will not hold water for anyone who denies logic. But this denial is very costly. If logical contradictions are not ultimately valid, then Suzuki must admit that assertions which directly contradict his can be equally as true (or false) as his own. If this is the case, then the statements, "God is all," "God stands outside the world order," and "There is no God," can each be equally true, and once again questions arise as to what one means by any particular statement.

If Watts were to allow the application of a logical criterion of plausibility to his world view, the results would be negative. Ultimately, although he applies the test of logical plausibility to other world views, uses logic in order to speak and write, and even rejects Christianity because of its logical implications for daily living, Watts would not allow a scrutiny of his system on logical grounds. For this reason, decisive internal criticism of his world view is difficult.

On the other hand, most human beings feel that the pantheistic world view cannot explain the human experience of the world as they have experienced it. Many who intuit strongly the validity of ordinary consciousness and its feeling of separate existence contend that pantheism does not (and cannot) adequately incorporate the intersubjectively verified experience of living as a personal, finite center of feeling, deciding and thinking. Because of these conceptual difficulties, many who understand the implications of pantheism feel that, as a world and life view, pantheism fails the test of logical plausibility.

NOTES

Chapter 1

[1]Plato, *The Republic* in *Great Dialogues of Plato*, ed. and trans. W. H. D. Rouse (New York: Mentor Books, 1956), pp. 402-03.

[2]Thomas E. Hosinski, "Science, Religion, and the Self-Understanding of Man," *Religion in Life* 42 (Summer 1973), pp. 179, 181.

[3]Alan Watts, *The Wisdom of Insecurity* (New York: Random House, Pantheon Books, 1951), p. 114.

[4]Paul Tillich, *My Search for Absolutes* (New York: Simon & Schuster, 1967), p. 142.

[5]C. S. Lewis, *Miracles* (London: Geoffrey Bles, 1947; rpt., 1959), p. 100.

[6]Alan Watts, *Behold the Spirit* (London: J. John Murray, 1947), pp. 80-81.

[7]Huxley popularized what was originally Leibniz's concept and terminology.

[8]Aldous Huxley, *The Perennial Philosophy* (New York: Harper & Bros., 1945), p. vii.

[9]Lawrence Watts, Foreword to *In My Own Way*, by Alan Watts (New York: Random House, Pantheon Books, 1972), p. vii.

[10]Alan Watts, *Myth and Ritual in Christianity* (London: Thames & Hudson, 1964), p. 21.

[11]Ibid., pp. xi-xii.

[12]Watts, *In My Own Way*, p. 209.

[13]Watts, *Beyond Theology*, p. 7.

[14]Ibid., p. 225.

[15]Alan Watts, *The Book: On the Taboo against Knowing Who You Are* (New York: Random House, Pantheon Books, 1966; rpt., P. F. Collier & Son, 1970), p. 137.

[16]William Johnston, *The Still Point: Reflections on Zen and Christian Mysticism* (New York: Fordham University Press, 1970), p. 164.

Chapter 2

[1]Johnston, *Still Point*, p. 165.

[2]For a complete discussion of the three basic laws of logic, see Irving M. Copi, *Introduction to Logic* (New York: Macmillan, 1972), pp. 284-86.

[3]Alan Watts, *Two Hands of God: The Myths of Polarity* (New York: George Braziller, 1963), pp. 4-5.

[4]Ibid., p. 185.

[5]Ibid., p. 49.

[6]Watts, *The Book*, pp. 46-47.

[7]Christmas Humphreys, *An Invitation to the Buddhist Way of Life for Western Readers* (New York: Schocken Books, 1969), p. 149.

[8]Watts, *The Book*, pp. 89-90.

[9]Watts, *Behold the Spirit*, pp. 145-46.

[10]Alan Watts, *The Joyous Cosmology: Adventures in the Chemistry of Consciousness* (New York: Random House, Vintage Books, 1962), p. 9.

[11]Watts, *Beyond Theology*, pp. 226-27.

[12]Watts, *The Book*, p. 93.

[13]Watts, *Two Hands of God*, pp. 17, 23-24.

[14]Watts, *The Book*, pp. 57, 82.

[15]Watts, *Behold the Spirit*, pp. 86-87.

[16]Watts, *Beyond Theology*, pp. 127-28.

[17]Ibid., p. 34.

[18]Ibid., pp. 70-71.

[19]Watts, *The Book*, p. 6.

[20]Watts, *Behold the Spirit*, p. 145.

[21]Watts, *Beyond Theology*, pp. 192-93.

[22]Watts, *Two Hands of God*, p. 183.

[23]Ibid., p. 28.

[24]Watts, *Beyond Theology*, p. 215.

[25]Watts, *Two Hands of God*, p. 17.

[26]Alan Watts, *Nature, Man and Woman* (New York: Random House, Pantheon Books, 1958), pp. 86-87.

[27]Watts, *Beyond Theology*, p. 34.

[28]Alan Watts, *Psychotherapy East and West* (New York: Random House, Pantheon Books, 1961), p. 133.

[29]Alan Watts, *Spirit of Zen* (New York: E. P. Dutton, 1936), p. 23.

[30]Watts, *Joyous Cosmology*, p. 4.

[31]Watts, *Beyond Theology*, pp. 154-55.

[32]Ibid., p. 213.

[33]Alan Watts, *This Is It* (New York: Random House, Pantheon Books, 1960; rpt. New York: P. F. Collier & Son, Collier Books, 1967), pp. 44-45.

[34]Watts, *The Book*, pp. 110-12.
[35]Ibid., p. 6.
[36]Ibid., p. 27.
[37]Watts, *Beyond Theology*, pp. 49-50.
[38]Watts, *The Book*, p. 6.
[39]Watts, *Beyond Theology*, p. 215.
[40]Watts, *Myth and Ritual*, p. 149.
[41]Watts, *Joyous Cosmology*, pp. 3-4.
[42]Watts, *Behold the Spirit*, p. 143.
[43]Sarvepalli Radhakrishnan, *The Hindu Way of Life* (New York: Macmillan, 1927; rpt. 1968), p. 51.
[44]Watts, *Beyond Theology*, p. 71.
[45]Watts, *Two Hands of God*, p. 55.
[46]Ibid., pp. 4-5.
[47]Ibid., p. 5.

Chapter 3
[1]Watts, *Behold the Spirit*, p. 9.
[2]Watts, *In My Own Way*, p. 207.
[3]Huxley, *Philosophia Perennis*, p. vii.
[4]Watts, *Behold the Spirit*, p. 9.
[5]Watts, *Beyond Theology*, pp. 15-16.
[6]Ibid., p. 205.
[7]Watts, *Myth and Ritual*, p. 136.
[8]Ibid.
[9]Watts, *Two Hands of God*, pp. 145-46.
[10]Watts, *Myth and Ritual*, p. 204.
[11]Watts, *Behold the Spirit*, p. 15.
[12]Ibid., pp. 20, 22.
[13]Alan Watts, *Cloud-hidden, Whereabouts Unknown* (New York: Random House, Pantheon Books, 1973), p. 130.
[14]Watts, *Behold the Spirit*, pp. 31, 202.
[15]Ibid., p. 145.
[16]Watts, *Myth and Ritual*, p. 128.
[17]Watts, *Beyond Theology*, p. 93.
[18]Watts, *Myth and Ritual*, p. 149.
[19]Watts, *Beyond Theology*, p. 151.
[20]Ibid., pp. 165-67.
[21]Ibid.
[22]Watts, *Spirit of Zen*, pp. 69-73.
[23]Watts, *Beyond Theology*, p. 136.
[24]Ibid., pp. xi-xii.
[25]Ibid.
[26]Watts, *In My Own Way*, p. 209.
[27]Watts, *Beyond Theology*, pp. 207-08.
[28]Watts, *The Book*, pp. 51, 56-57.
[29]Watts, *Beyond Theology*, p. 223.

[30]Watts, *Cloud-hidden,* p. 129.

[31]Watts, *Beyond Theology,* pp. 108, 112, 115.

[32]Alan Watts, *Does It Matter?* (New York: Random House, Pantheon Books, 1970), p. 103.

[33]Watts, *Wisdom of Insecurity,* pp. 145-46.

[34]Watts, *Cloud-hidden,* pp. 138-39.

[35]Ibid.

[36]Watts, *Beyond Theology,* p. 136.

[37]Ibid., p. 113.

[38]Watts, *Wisdom of Insecurity,* pp. 137, 139-40.

[39]Watts, *Myth and Ritual,* p. 234.

[40]Watts, *Wisdom of Insecurity,* p. 24.

[41]Watts, *Spirit of Zen,* p. 55.

[42]Watts, *In My Own Way,* p. 207.

[43]D. T. Suzuki, *Mysticism: Christian and Buddhist* (New York: Harper & Bros., 1957; rpt. New York: Crowel-Collier, Collier Books, 1962), pp. 11, 16.

[44]Watts, *Beyond Theology,* p. 220.

[45]Ibid., p. 222.

[46]Ibid., pp. 223-25.

[47]Paul Tillich, *Christianity and the Encounter of the World Religions* (New York: Columbia, 1963), p. 28.

[48]Watts, *In My Own Way,* pp. 211-12.

[49]Watts, *Beyond Theology,* p. 208.

Chapter 4

[1]Watts, *Behold the Spirit,* p. 79.

[2]Christmas Humphreys, *Zen Buddhism* (London: William Heinemann, 1949; rpt. London: Allen & Unwin, Unwin Books, 1961), p. 13.

[3]Watts, *Spirit of Zen,* pp. 15-16.

[4]Henri Benoit, *The Supreme Doctrine,* trans. T. Gray (New York: Random House, Pantheon Books, 1955; rpt. New York: Viking Press, Compass Books, 1959), p. xiv.

[5]R. H. Blyth, *Zen in English Literature and Oriental Classics* (Tokyo: Hokuseido Press, 1942; rpt. New York: E. P. Dutton, 1960), p. 170.

[6]Watts, *Spirit of Zen,* p. 16.

[7]Watts, *Beyond Theology,* pp. 212-13.

[8]Ibid.

[9]Humphreys, *Zen Buddhism,* p. 26.

[10]Watts, *Myth and Ritual,* p. 15.

[11]Blyth, *Zen in Literature,* p. 180.

[12]Watts, *Behold the Spirit,* p. 132.

[13]Watts, *Spirit of Zen,* pp. 62, 64.

[14]Ibid.

[15]Ibid., p. 17.

[16]Watts, *Psychotherapy East and West,* p. 147.

[17]Johnston, *Still Point,* p. 84.

[18]D. T. Suzuki, *Zen Buddhism: Selected Writings*, ed. William Barrett (Garden City: Doubleday & Co., Anchor Books, 1956), p. 105.
[19]Watts, *Psychotherapy East and West*, pp. 129, 137-38.
[20]Watts, *Myth and Ritual*, p. 182.
[21]Suzuki, *Zen Buddhism*, p. 84.
[22]Watts, *Spirit of Zen*, pp. 60-61.
[23]Ibid.
[24]Ibid., p. 67.
[25]Watts, *Wisdom of Insecurity*, pp. 142-43.
[26]Watts, *Spirit of Zen*, p. 44.
[27]Watts, *Myth and Ritual*, p. 234.
[28]Watts, *Behold the Spirit*, p. 76.
[29]Eugene Wehrli, *The Gospel and Conflicting Faiths* (Boston: United Church Press, 1969), pp. 180-81.
[30]Suzuki, *Mysticism*, p. 28.
[31]Ibid., p. 17.
[32]Stephen Neill, *Christian Faith and Other Faiths* (London: Oxford University Press, 1961), pp. 112-13.
[33]For a discussion of substantial views of mind, see Harold H. Titus, *Living Issues in Philosophy* (New York: D. Van Nostrand, 1970), pp. 164-65.
[34]*Chicago Daily News*, 17-18 November 1973, p. 26.
[35]Clare, D. Kinsman, ed., *Contemporary Authors*, vols. 41-44 (Detroit: Gale Research, 1974), p. 669.
[36]Watts, *Myth and Ritual*, p. 15.
[37]Watts, *Wisdom of Insecurity*, pp. 142-43.
[38]Watts, *Spirit of Zen*, pp. 19-20.
[39]Suzuki, *Mysticism*, p. 49.

Chapter 5
[1]Thomas Merton, *Mystics and Zen Masters* (New York: Farrar, Straus & Giroux, 1967), p. 13.
[2]Basil Mitchell, *The Justification of Religious Belief*, Philosophy of Religion Series (New York: Seabury Press, Crossroad Books, 1973), pp. 62-63, 67.
[3]Watts, *Beyond Theology*, pp. 12-13.
[4]Watts, *Myth and Ritual*, p. 21.
[5]Watts, *Beyond Theology*, pp. 207-208.
[6]Ibid.
[7]Ibid.
[8]Watts, *The Book*, p. 57.
[9]Robert Flint, *Anti-Theistic Theories* (London: Wm. Blackwood & Sons, 1899), p. 431.
[10]Ibid.
[11]Neill, *Christian Faith*, p. 113.
[12]H. P. Owen, *Concepts of Deity*, Philosophy of Religion Series (New York: Herder & Herder, 1971), p. 70.

[13]Norman Geisler, *Philosophy of Religion* (Grand Rapids: Zondervan, 1974), p. 217.

[14]Watts, *Beyond Theology*, p. 19.

[15]Owen, *Concepts of Deity*, p. 70.

[16]Ibid., p. 217.

[17]Watts, *Beyond Theology*, p. 215.

[18]Flint, *Anti-Theistic Theories*, p. 396.

[19]Watts, *Behold the Spirit*, p. 139.

[20]Watts, *Wisdom of Insecurity*, p. 114.

[21]See pp. 60-62.

[22]Norman Geisler, *Apologetics* (Grand Rapids: Baker Book House, 1976), pp. 188-89.

[23]Watts, *Behold the Spirit*, p. 132.

[24]Owen, *Concepts of Deity*, pp. 69-70.

[25]Huxley, *Philosophia Perennis*, p. vii.

[26]It should be noted that when Watts rejected Christianity, he did not give up the *Philosophia Perennis* just because the universality of its support was diminished somewhat. In later years, however, he emphasized the personal application of, not the universal support for, the pantheistic world view. See p. 62.

[27]Watts, *Behold the Spirit*, pp. 86-87.

[28]William James, *Varieties of Religious Experience* (New York: Longmans, Green & Co., 1902; rpt. New York: Random House, The Modern Library, 1929), p. 399.

[29]Frederick Ferré, *Basic Modern Philosophy of Religion* (New York: Scribner's Sons, 1967), p. 102.

[30]Quoted in R. C. Zaehner, *Zen, Drugs and Mysticism* (New York: Random House, Pantheon Books, 1972), pp. 108-109.

[31]Watts, *Behold the Spirit, The Supreme Identity* and *Myth and Ritual in Christianity*.

[32]Watts, *Beyond Theology*, p. vii.

[33]Ibid.

[34]Watts, *Cloud-hidden*, p. 132.

[35]Watts, *Myth and Ritual*, p. 230.

[36]Watts, *The Book*, p. 57.

[37]Ibid., p. 6.

[38]Georgia Harkness, *Mysticism: Its Meaning and Message* (Nashville: Abingdon Press, 1973), p. 72.

[39]Radhakrishnan, *Hindu Life*, p. 19.

[40]James, *Varieties*, p. 414.

[41]F. R. Tennant, *Philosophical Theology*, vol. 1 (Cambridge: Cambridge University Press, 1956), p. 317.

[42]Martin Buber, *The Eclipse of God*, trans. M. S. Friedman, et. al. (New York: Harper & Bros., 1952), p. 154.

[43]Zaehner, *Zen, Drugs and Mysticism*, p. 109.

[44]Watts, *Myth and Ritual*, p. 15.

[45]Ibid.

[46]Walter T. Stace, *Mysticism and Philosophy* (Philadelphia: Lippincott, 1960), p. 297.

[47]Harkness, *Mysticism*, p. 71.

[48]Tennant, *Philosophical Theology*, pp. 319-20.

[49]James, *Varieties*, p. 417.

[50]James deals primarily with the "core" of *religious* experience, not with the "core" of *mystical* experience. Part of the "core" of religious experience (namely, the reality of Transcendence as over against this immanent sphere) goes against what most pantheistic mystics would claim as the result of their experience.

[51]Ferré, *Philosophy of Religion*, p. 102.

[52]Watts, *Wisdom of Insecurity*, p. 114.

[53]Flint, *Anti-Theistic Theories*, p. 411.

[54]Watts, *Wisdom of Insecurity*, pp. 43-44.

Chapter 6

[1]Stuart Hackett, *Resurrection of Theism* (Chicago: Moody Press, 1957), p. 247.

[2]A similar dilemma is elaborated more fully in Hackett's *Resurrection of Theism*, pp. 246-50.

[3]Quoted in Watts, *Behold the Spirit*, p. 114.

[4]Suzuki, *Mysticism*, p. 49.

[5]Watts, *Behold the Spirit*, p. 114.

[6]Watts, *Wisdom of Insecurity*, p. 142.

[7]Watts, *Behold the Spirit*, p. 146.

[8]Ibid., pp. 139-40.

[9]Watts, *Nature, Man and Woman*, p. ix.

[10]Watts, *The Book*, p. 20.

[11]Humphreys, *Zen Buddhism*, p. 158.

[12]Tennant, *Philosophical Theology*, p. 317.

[13]Suzuki, *Mysticism*, p. 49.

BIBLIOGRAPHY

Anderson, J. N. D. *Christianity and Comparative Religion*. Downers Grove: InterVarsity Press, 1970.

Benoit, Henri. *The Supreme Doctrine*. Trans. T. Gray. New York: Random House, Pantheon Books, 1955; rpt. New York: Viking Press, Compass Books, 1959.

Blyth, R. H. *Zen in English Literature and Oriental Classics*. Tokyo: Hokuseido Press, 1942; rpt. New York: E. P. Dutton & Co., Dutton Paperback, 1960.

Buber, Martin. *The Eclipse of God*. Trans. M. S. Friedman, N. Guterman, E. Kameuka and I. M. Lask. New York: Harper & Bros., 1952.

Butler, Dom Edward Cuthbert. *Western Mysticism*. London: Constable & Co., 1922.

Eckhart, Meister. *Meister Eckhart: A Modern Translation*. Ed. and trans. by R. B. Blakney. New York: Harper & Bros., 1941.

Ferré, Frederick. *Basic Modern Philosophy of Religion*. New York: Scribner's Sons, 1967.

Flint, Robert. *Anti-Theistic Theories*. London: William Blackwood & Sons, 1899.

Geisler, Norman. *Philosophy of Religion*. Grand Rapids: Zondervan, 1974.

Hackett, Stuart. *The Resurrection of Theism*. Chicago: Moody, 1957.

Harkness, Georgia. *Mysticism: Its Meaning and Message*. Nashville: Abingdon, 1973.

Humphreys, Christmas. *An Invitation to the Buddhist Way of Life for Western Readers*. New York: Schocken Books, 1969.

_____. *Zen Buddhism*. London: William Heinemann, 1949; rpt. London: Allen & Unwin, 1961.

Hunt, John. *Pantheism and Christianity*. Port Washington: Kennikat, 1884; rpt. 1970.

Huxley, Aldous. *The Perennial Philosophy*. New York: Harper & Bros., 1945.

Inge, William Ralph. *Christian Mysticism*. New York: Chas. Scribner's Sons, 1899.

James, William. *Varieties of Religious Experience*. New York: Longmans, Green & Co., 1902; rpt. New York: Random House, The Modern Library, 1929.

Johnston, William. *The Still Point: Reflections on Zen and Christian Mysticism*. New York: Fordham University Press, 1970.

_____. "Zen and Christian Mysticism: A Study in Comparative Psychology." *International Philosophical Quarterly*, 7, (1967), 441-69.

Kraemer, Hendrik. *The Christian Message in a Non-Christian World*. New York: International Missionary Council, 1938; rpt. Grand Rapids: Kregel Publications, 1956.

Lewis, C. S. *Miracles*. London: Geoffrey Bles, 1947; rpt., 1959.

Masters, R. E. L. and Houston, Jean. *The Varieties of Psychedelic Experience*. New York: Holt, Rinehart & Winston, 1966.

Merton, Thomas. *Mystics and Zen Masters*. New York: Farrar, Straus & Giroux, 1967.

Mitchell, Basil. *The Justification of Religious Belief*. New York: Seabury Press, Crossroad Books, 1973.

Neill, Stephen. *Christian Faith and Other Faiths*. London: Oxford University Press, 1961.

Otto, Rudolf. *Mysticism East and West*. Trans. B. L. Bracey and R. C. Payne. New York: Macmillan, 1932.

Owen, H. P. *Concepts of Deity*. New York: Herder & Herder, 1971.

Parrinder, Geoffrey. *Upanishads, Gītā, and Bible*. London: Faber & Faber, 1962.

Radhakrishnan, Sarvepalli. *Eastern Religions and Western Thought*. Oxford: Clarendon, 1940.

_____. *The Hindu Way of Life*. New York: Macmillan, 1927; rpt., 1968.

Riepe, Dale. "The Indian Influence in American Philosophy." *Philosophy East and West* 17 (1967), 125-37.

Roszak, Theodore. *The Making of a Counter Culture*. Garden City: Doubleday & Co., Anchor Books, 1969.

Schaeffer, Francis A. *The God Who Is There*. Chicago: InterVarsity Press, 1968.

Soper, Edmund Davison. *The Inevitable Choice: Vedanta Philosophy or Christian Gospel*. New York: Abingdon Press, 1957.

Stace, Walter Terence. *Mysticism and Philosophy*. Philadelphia: Lippincott, 1960.

Suligoj, Herman F. "The Mystical Philosophy of Alan Watts." *International Philosophical Quarterly* 15 (1975), 439-54.

Suzuki, D. T. *Mysticism: Christian and Buddhist*. New York: Harper & Bros., 1957; rpt. New York: Crowel-Collier, Collier Books, 1962.

————. *Zen Buddhism: Selected Writings*. Ed. William Barrett. Garden City: Doubleday & Co., Anchor Books, 1956.

Tennant, F. R. *Philosophical Theology*. Vol. I. Cambridge: Cambridge University Press, 1928; rpt., 1956.

Tillich, Paul. *Christianity and the Encounter of the World Religions*. New York: Columbia University Press, 1963.

Watts, Alan Wilson. *The Art of Contemplation*. New York: Random House, Pantheon Books, 1972.

————. *Beat Zen, Square Zen and Zen*. San Francisco: City Lights Books, 1959.

————. *Behold the Spirit*. London: J. John Murray, 1947.

————. *Beyond Theology: The Art of Godmanship*. Toronto: Random House, Pantheon Books, 1964.

————. *The Book: On the Taboo against Knowing Who You Are*. New York: Random House, Pantheon Books, 1966; rpt. P. F. Collier & Son, 1970.

————. *Cloud-hidden, Whereabouts Unknown*. New York: Random House, Pantheon Books, 1973.

————. *The Cosmic Drama*. Essence of Alan Watts Series, no. 9. Milbrae, Cal.: Celestial Arts, 1974.

————. *Death*. Essence of Alan Watts Series, no. 4. Milbrae, Cal.: Celestial Arts, 1974.

————. *Does It Matter?* New York: Random House, Pantheon Books, 1970.

————. *Easter, Its Story and Meaning*. Great Religious Festivals Series, no. 4. New York: Henry Schuman, 1950.

————. *Ego*. Essence of Alan Watts Series, no. 8. Milbrae, Cal.: Celestial Arts, 1974.

————. *Erotic Spirituality: The Vision of Konarak*. New York: Macmillan, 1971.

————. *God*. Essence of Alan Watts Series, no. 1. Milbrae, Cal.: Celestial Arts, 1973.

————. *In My Own Way*. New York: Random House, Pantheon Books, 1972.

————. *The Joyous Cosmology: Adventures in the Chemistry of Consciousness*. Foreword by Timothy Leary and Richard Alpert. New York: Random House, Vintage Books, 1962.

————. *The Legacy of Asia and Western Man*. London: J. John Murray, 1937.

————. *Meaning of Happiness*. New York: Harper and Row, 1940.

————. *Meditation*. Essence of Alan Watts Series, no. 2. Milbrae, Cal.: Celestial Arts, 1974.

————. *Myth and Ritual in Christianity*. Myth and Man Series. London: Thames & Hudson, 1954.

————. *Nature, Man and Woman*. New York: Random House, Pantheon

Books, 1958.
_____. *The Nature of Man.* Essence of Alan Watts Series, no. 5. Milbrae, Cal.: Celestial Arts, 1974.
_____. *Nothingness.* Essence of Alan Watts Series, no. 3. Milbrae, Cal.: Celestial Arts, 1974.
_____. *Philosophical Fantasies.* Essence of Alan Watts Series, no. 7. Milbrae, Cal.: Celestial Arts, 1974.
_____. *Psychotherapy East and West.* New York: Random House, Pantheon Books, 1961.
_____. *Seven Symbols of Life.* London: Buddhist Lodge, 1936.
_____. *Spirit of Zen.* New York: E. P. Dutton & Co., 1936.
_____. *The Supreme Identity.* New York: Random House, Pantheon Books, 1950; rpt., 1972.
_____. *Tao: The Watercourse Way.* New York: Random House, Pantheon Books, 1975.
_____. *This Is It.* New York: Random House, Pantheon Books, 1960; rpt. New York: Collier & Son, Collier Books, 1967.
_____. *Time.* Essence of Alan Watts Series, no. 6. Milbrae, Cal.: Celestial Arts, 1974.
_____. *Two Hands of God: The Myths of Polarity.* New York: George Braziller, 1963.
_____. *The Way of Liberation in Zen Buddhism.* Asian Study Monographs, no. 1. San Francisco: American Academy of Asian Studies, 1955.
_____. *The Way of Zen.* New York: Random House, Pantheon Books, 1957.
_____. *The Wisdom of Insecurity: A Message for an Age of Anxiety.* New York: Random House, Pantheon Books, 1951; rpt. Random House, Vintage Books, 1968.
_____. *Zen.* Stanford: James Ladd Delkin, 1948.
_____. *Zen Buddhism.* London: Buddhist Society, 1947.
Wehrli, Eugene S. *The Gospel and Conflicting Faiths.* Boston: United Church Press, 1969.
Zaehner, Robert C. *Mysticism, Sacred and Profane.* Oxford: Clarendon Press, 1957; rpt. Oxford: Oxford University Press, Oxford Paperbacks, 1961.
_____. *Zen, Drugs and Mysticism.* New York: Random House, Pantheon Books, 1972.

DATE DUE